NETSCAPE
NAVIGATOR 3

AN INTRODUCTION

Gary B. Shelly
Thomas J. Cashman
Kurt A. Jordan

COURSE TECHNOLOGY
ONE MAIN STREET
CAMBRIDGE MA 02142

an International Thomson Publishing company   I⊤P*

CAMBRIDGE • ALBANY • BONN • CINCINNATI • LONDON • MADRID • MELBOURNE

MEXICO CITY • NEW YORK • PARIS • SAN FRANCISCO • TOKYO • TORONTO • WASHINGTON

SHELLY
CASHMAN
SERIES®

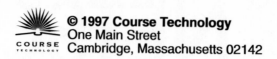

© 1997 Course Technology
One Main Street
Cambridge, Massachusetts 02142

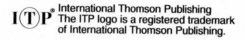

International Thomson Publishing
The ITP logo is a registered trademark
of International Thomson Publishing.

Printed in the United States of America

For more information, contact Course Technology:

Course Technology
One Main Street
Cambridge, Massachusetts 02142, USA

International Thomson Editores
Campos Eliseos 385, Piso 7
Colonia Polanco
11560 Mexico D.F. Mexico

International Thomson Publishing Europe
Berkshire House
168-173 High Holborn
London, WC1V 7AA, United Kingdom

International Thomson Publishing GmbH
Konigswinterer Strasse 418
53227 Bonn, Germany

Thomas Nelson Australia
102 Dodds Street
South Melbourne
Victoria 3205 Australia

International Thomson Publishing Asia
Block 211, Henderson Road #08-03
Henderson Industrial Park
Singapore 0315

Nelson Canada
1120 Birchmont Road
Scarborough, Ontario
Canada M1K 5G4

International Thomson Publishing Japan
Hirakawa-cho Kyowa Building, 3F
2-2-1 Hirakawa-cho, Chiyoda-ku
Tokyo 102, Japan

ISBN 0-7895-1280-7

PHOTO CREDITS: *Project 1, page NN 1.4,* Computer Man provided by PhotoDisc Inc. ©1996; Sputnik, Courtesy of UPI/BETTMAN;
Project 2, pages NN 2.2-3, Airplane and globe, gold bars, computer, books, and magnifying glass, Courtesy of Corel Professional Photos
CD-ROM Image usage; *Project 3, pages NN 3.2-3,* Snail, stamp, and mailbox, Courtesy of Corel Professional Photos CD-ROM Image usage

6 7 8 9 10 BC 10 9 8 7

NETSCAPE
NAVIGATOR 3

AN INTRODUCTION

CONTENTS

Preface

Shelly Cashman Series®

The Shelly Cashman Series® offers superior materials from which to learn about computers. The Shelly Cashman Series includes computer concepts, personal computer applications, programming, networking, and World Wide Web access. The books are available in a variety of traditionally bound textbooks or in the Shelly Cashman Series unique Custom Edition® program, which allows you to choose from a number of options and create a textbook perfectly suited to your course.

Using this textbook reinforces the fact that you make the right choice with a Shelly Cashman Series book. Textbooks in the Shelly Cashman Series have been thoroughly redesigned to present material in an even easier to understand format. Features such as Other Ways and More About were added to give in-depth knowledge to the student. The opening of each project provides a fascinating perspective of the subject covered in the project. Completely redesigned student assignments include the unique Cases and Places. This book provides the finest educational experience ever for a student learning about computer software.

The World Wide Web

In just seven years since its birth, the World Wide Web, or Web for short, has grown beyond all expectations. Within only a few years, the Web has increased from a limited number of networked computers to hundreds of thousands of computers offering millions of Web pages on any topic you can imagine. Schools, businesses, and the computing industry all are taking advantage of this new way of accessing the Internet to provide products, services, and education electronically. Netscape Navigator 3 provides the novice as well as the experienced user a window with which to look into the Web and tap an abundance of resources. All are available at the click of a mouse button. The World Wide Web is within reach of anyone with a computer, modem, and the proper software. Thus, an up-to-date educational institution that teaches students how to use computers must teach Web basics.

Educational and charitable nonprofit institutions can obtain Netscape Navigator 3 for classroom use without cost. For more information, call (415) 528-2555.

Objectives of This Textbook

Netscape Navigator 3: An Introduction is intended for use in combination with other books in an introductory computer concepts course or in a personal computer applications course. Specific objectives of this book are as follows:

- ▶ To expose the student to various World Wide Web resources
- ▶ To teach the student how to use Netscape Navigator 3 to access the World Wide Web
- ▶ To acquaint the student with the more popular search engines
- ▶ To teach the student how to communicate with other Internet users

> ▶ To encourage curiosity and independent exploration of World Wide Web resources

> ▶ To develop an exercise-oriented approach that allows the student to learn by example

Organization of This Textbook

Netscape Navigator 3: An Introduction consists of three projects and an appendix that introduce the student to the World Wide Web. Neither World Wide Web nor Internet experience is necessary. Each project begins with a statement of objectives. The topics in the project are presented in a step-by-step, screen-by-screen manner.

Each project ends with a Project Summary and a section titled What You Should Know. Questions and exercises are presented at the end of each project. Exercises include Test Your Knowledge, Use Help, and In the Lab. The projects conclude with the unique Cases and Places. The projects and appendix are organized as follows.

Project 1 – Introduction to Netscape   In Project 1, students are introduced to the World Wide Web and its components. Topics include how the Web is organized; URLs; browsing Web pages; Web page management techniques; saving and printing material obtained from a Web site; and using Netscape Help.

Project 2 – Information Mining Using Web Search Engines   In Project 2, students begin to explore the potential of the World Wide Web. Topics include techniques for searching the vast amount of materials available on the Web using search engines such as Infoseek, AltaVista, WebCrawler, Lycos, and Yahoo and using traditional Internet services such as FTP and gopher via Netscape.

Project 3 – Conversing Over the Internet   In Project 3, students are introduced to the various techniques for communicating with other Web users around the world. Topics include sending and receiving electronic mail; mail management techniques; reading and posting newsgroup articles; conversing using WebChat; and participating in Internet Relay Chat conversations using NetChat.

Appendix A – Popular Web Sites   Appendix A lists the URLs of popular Web sites organized into categories. Topics include art; business; entertainment; government; Internet Relay Chat; job opportunities; miscellaneous; museums; music; news/periodicals; shopping; sports; and FTP and gopher sites.

End-of-Project Student Activities

A notable strength of the Shelly Cashman Series Internet books is the extensive student activities at the end of each project. Well-structured student activities can make the difference between students merely participating in a class and students retaining the information they learn. These activities include all of the following sections.

> ▶ **What You Should Know**   A listing of the tasks completed within a project together with the pages where the step-by-step, screen-by-screen explanations appear. This section provides a perfect study review for the student.

> ▶ **Test Your Knowledge**   Four pencil-and-paper activities designed to determine the student's understanding of the material in the project. Included are true/false questions, multiple-choice questions, and two short-answer exercises.

▶ **Use Help**   Any user of Netscape Navigator must know how to use Help. Therefore, this books contains two Help exercises per project. These exercises alone distinguish the Shelly Cashman Series from any other set of instructional materials.

▶ **In the Lab**   Several assignments per project that require the student to apply the knowledge gained in the project to solve problems.

▶ **Cases and Places**   Seven unique case studies allow students to apply their knowledge to real-world situations.

Instructor's Resource Kit

A comprehensive Instructor's Resource Kit (IRK) accompanies this textbook in the form of a CD-ROM. The CD-ROM includes an electronic Instructor's Manual (called ElecMan) and teaching and testing aids. The CD-ROM (ISBN 0-7895-1273-4) is available through your Course Technology representative or by calling 1-800-648-7450. The contents of the CD-ROM are listed below.

▶ **ElecMan (Electronic Instructor's Manual)**   ElecMan is made up of Microsoft Word files. The files include lecture notes, solutions to laboratory assignments, and a large test bank. The files allow you to modify the lecture notes or generate quizzes and exams from the test bank using you own word processor. ElecMan includes the following for each project: project objectives; project overview; detailed lesson plans with page number references; teacher notes and activities; answers to the end-of-project exercises; test bank of 110 questions (50 true/false, 25 multiple-choice, and 35 fill-in-the blanks); transparency references; and selected transparencies. The transparencies are available on the Figures on CD-ROM described below. The test bank questions are numbered the same as in Course Test Manager. Thus, you can print a copy of the project and use the printed test bank to select your questions in Course Test Manager.

▶ **Figures on CD-ROM**   Illustrations for every screen in the textbook are available. Use this ancillary to create a slide show from the illustrations for lecture or to print transparencies for use in lecture with an overhead.

▶ **Course Test Manager**   This cutting-edge Windows-based testing software helps instructors design and administer tests and pre-tests. The full-featured online program permits students to take tests at the computer where their grades are computed immediately following completion of the exam. Automatic statistics collection, student guides customized to the student's performance, and printed tests are only a few of the features.

▶ **Lecture Success System**   The Lecture Success System is a set of files that allows you to explain and illustrate the step-by-step, screen-by-screen development of a project in the textbook without an Internet connection. In lecture, students will not know the difference between using the files and an Internet connection, except that the Web pages will display instantaneously with the Lecture Success System. The Lecture Success System requires that you have a copy of Netscape Navigator, a personal computer, and a projection device.

▶ **Interactive Labs**   Fourteen hands-on interactive labs that take the student from ten to fifteen minutes to step through help solidify and reinforce computer concepts. Student assessment requires the student to answer questions about the contents of the interactive labs.

Shelly Cashman Online

Shelly Cashman Online is a World Wide Web service available to instructors and students of computer education. Visit Shelly Cashman Online at http://www.scseries.com. Shelly Cashman Online is divided into four areas:

▶ **Series Information**   Information on the Shelly Cashman Series products.

▶ **The Community**   Opportunities to discuss your course and your ideas with instructors in your field and with the Shelly Cashman Series team.

▶ **Teaching Resources**   This area includes password-protected data, course outlines, teaching tips, and ancillaries such as ElecMan.

▶ **Student Center**   Dedicated to students learning about computers with Shelly Cashman Series textbooks and software. This area includes cool links and much more.

Acknowledgments

The Shelly Cashman Series would not be the leading computer education series without the contributions of outstanding publishing professionals. First, and foremost, among them is Becky Herrington, director of production and designer. She is the heart and soul of the Shelly Cashman Series, and it is only through her leadership, dedication, and tireless efforts that superior products are made possible. Becky created and produced the award-winning Windows 95 series of books.

Under Becky's direction, the following individuals made significant contributions to this book. Peter Schiller, production manager; Ginny Harvey, series administrator and manuscript editor; Ken Russo, senior illustrator; Mike Bodnar, Stephanie Nance, and Dave Bonnewitz, Quark artists and illustrators; Patti Garbarino, editorial assistant; Jeanne Black, Quark expert; Nancy Lamm, proofreader; Cristina Haley, indexer; and Jim Quasney, series editor.

Gary B. Shelly
Thomas J. Cashman
Kurt A. Jordan

Visit Shelly Cashman Online at
http://www.scseries.com

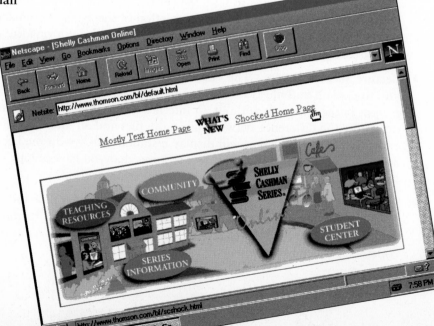

Netscape Navigator 3

Windows 95

Introduction to Netscape

Objectives:

You will have mastered the material in this project when you can:

▶ Define the Internet
▶ Describe hypermedia and browsers
▶ Explain a hypermedia link
▶ Start Netscape
▶ Describe Netscape features
▶ Maneuver through the history list
▶ Create and remove bookmarks
▶ Save Web pages on a floppy disk
▶ Print Web pages
▶ Save graphic images on a floppy disk
▶ Print graphic images
▶ Copy and paste from Web pages using the Clipboard
▶ Use Netscape online Help features

Surf's Up!
Catch the Internet Wave

The Internet is everywhere in our lives. From the White House to the Vatican, computer users worldwide can access a vast collection of information, both trite and monumental, that belongs to everyone, yet has no single owner.

The foundation was laid for this Information Superhighway in 1957 when Russia launched Sputnik, the first artificial Earth satellite. After the launch, the U.S. Department of Defense rushed to develop the first parts of a network to connect military sites, defense contractors, and research universities. The goal was simple: form an inviolable method of communication that would withstand nuclear bombing. The system was designed to be decentralized, meaning any part of it could be disabled and yet allow information to be transmitted via the routes that were still operable.

Based on these requirements, the Pentagon's Advanced Research Projects Agency unveiled ARPANET. In 1969, four computers were networked

Information Superhi

and able to communicate and share information and resources. By 1971, fifteen computers were in place, and in 1972, the number increased to 37. Thus, the network is a result of America's determination to be able to communicate in a post-nuclear world.

In the 1970s, more nonmilitary users were permitted to connect to ARPANET. By the 1980s, some networks began offering public access. Realizing that ARPANET was serving more than military needs, in 1983, the Department of Defense developed a separate network, Milnet, for its information. The remaining information stayed on ARPANET. As additional networks joined ARPANET, the term, Internet, originated to refer to this growing resource.

In 1991, the World Wide Web, or WWW, was introduced. Engineered and designed at the European Particle Physics Laboratory, the World Wide Web contains areas, called sites, with links that enable users to jump from site to site easily. Basically a universal database and a subset of the Internet, the World Wide Web currently is the most popular method of information retrieval on the Internet. Its popularity is due in large part to its capability of displaying information in a variety of formats including video and sound, as well as its ease of use. By clicking hypertext links, a user, affectionately called a surfer, quickly can jump to related resources.

As its name implies, the World Wide Web is, truly, worldwide. It is growing at an estimated one percent *each day*. While the World Wide Web is popular, the Internet is its backbone, however. With its exponential growth, it is difficult to determine how many people are connected to the Internet, but estimates range to more than three million. The number of users grows steadily at about ten percent per month.

With so much information available on the Internet, something exists for everyone. The projects you will complete in this book will show you how to use Netscape to access these resources. In no time, you will be joining the ranks of WWW aficionados and surfing the Net like a pro.

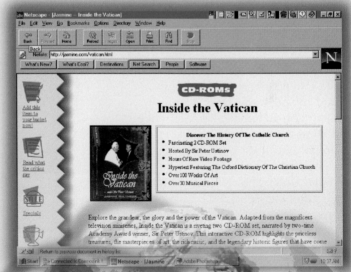

Project

Netscape Navigator 3

Windows 95

Introduction to Netscape

Introduction

Little known a few years ago, the Internet now is one of the more popular and faster growing areas in computing today. Using the Internet, you can do research, get a loan, shop for services and merchandise, look for a job, display weather maps, obtain pictures, movies, audio clips, and information stored on computers around the world, and converse with people worldwide.

Once considered mysterious, the Internet is now accessible to the general public because personal computers with user-friendly tools have reduced its complexity. The Internet, with hundreds of thousands of connected computers, continues to grow with thousands of new users coming online every month. Schools, businesses, newspapers, television stations, and government services can all be found on the Internet. Service providers are popping up all over the country providing inexpensive access to the Internet from the home; but just what exactly is the Internet?

Definition of the Internet

The **Internet** is a collection of networks (Figure 1-1), each of which is composed of a collection of smaller networks. For example, on a college campus, the network in the student lab can be connected to the faculty computer network, which is connected to the administration network, and they all can connect to the Internet.

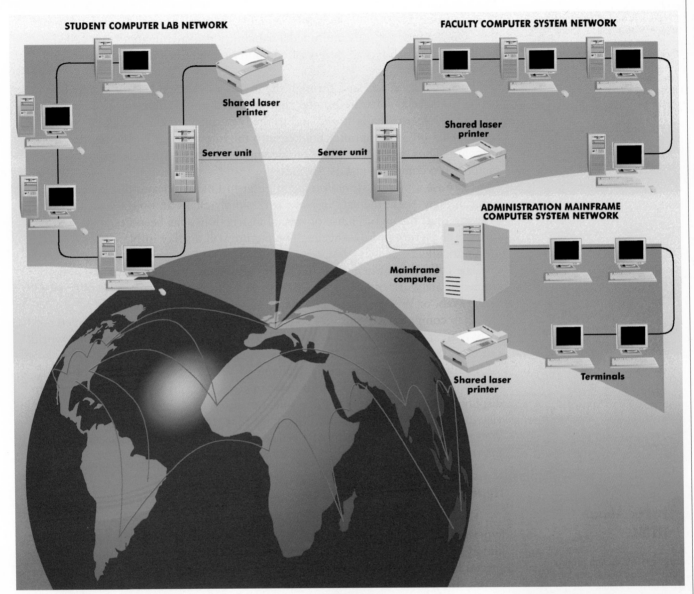

STUDENT COMPUTER LAB NETWORK

FACULTY COMPUTER SYSTEM NETWORK

Shared laser
printer

Server unit   Server unit

Shared laser
printer

ADMINISTRATION MAINFRAME
COMPUTER SYSTEM NETWORK

Mainframe
computer

Shared laser
printer

Terminals

FIGURE 1-1

Networks are connected with high-, medium- and low-speed data lines
that allow data to move from one computer to another. The separate networks
connect to the Internet through computers. An Internet connection from your
home would connect to an Internet service provider's computer over a low-speed
phone line. The provider's computer accesses the Internet over a high-speed line
to accommodate the many low-speed connections of its customers.

◆ **More** *About* **the Internet**

The Internet started as a government experiment for the military. The military wanted a communication technique that would connect different computers running different operating systems. This method had to survive when one or more of the computers became unavailable. From this experiment, a communication technique originated called Transmission Control Protocol/ Internet Protocol, or TCP/IP.

World Wide Web

Modern computer systems have the capability to deliver information in a variety of ways, such as graphics, sound, video clips, animation, and, of course, regular text. On the Internet, this multimedia capability is available in a form called **hypermedia**, which is any variety of computer media, including text, graphics, video, and sound.

Hypermedia is accessed through the use of a **hypertext link**, or simply **link**, which is a special software pointer that points to the location of the computer on which the hypermedia is stored and to the hypermedia itself. A link can point to hypermedia on any computer hooked into the Internet that is running the proper software. Thus, a hypertext link on a computer in New York can point to a picture on a computer in Los Angeles.

To cause a picture stored on a computer in Los Angeles to display on a computer in New York, the user in New York simply clicks an object such as text or a drawing that, through the use of special instructions, has been designated as a link to the picture in Los Angeles. The picture will display in New York automatically.

The collection of hypertext links throughout the Internet creates an interconnected network of links called the **World Wide Web**, which also is referred to as the **Web**, or **WWW**.

Each computer within the Web containing hypermedia that can be referenced by hypertext links is called a **Web site**. Thousands of Web sites around the world can be accessed through the Internet.

Pictures or other hypermedia available at Web sites are stored in files called **documents**, or **Web pages**. Therefore, when you click a hypertext linked object to display a picture, read text, view a video, or listen to a song, you are actually viewing a Web page or part of a Web page that contains the hypermedia. Each Web page has a unique address that identifies it from all other pages on the Internet.

Hypertext Markup Language

The authors of Web pages use a special formatting language, called **hypertext markup language**, or **html**, to create them. Behind all that formatted text and eye-catching graphics is plain text. The text and pictures are surrounded by special html formatting codes and functions that control such things as font size, colors, and centering. You can see the html used to create a Web page by clicking Document Source on the View menu. Figure 1-2 shows the hypertext markup language used to create the Web page shown in Figure 1-3. After browsing through the document source, you can return to the home page window by clicking the Close button in the upper right-hand corner of the screen.

Though it looks somewhat cryptic, html is similar to a computer programming language. Using html, it is possible for you to create your own Web pages and place them on the Web for others to see.

More *About*
Web Sites

An organization can have more than one Web site. Individual departments may have Web computers, allowing faster response to requests for Web pages and local control over the Web pages stored at that Web site.

More *About*
HTML

There are HTML editing programs, such as Hotdog and Hotmetal, that make it easy to create Web pages without having to learn HTML syntax.

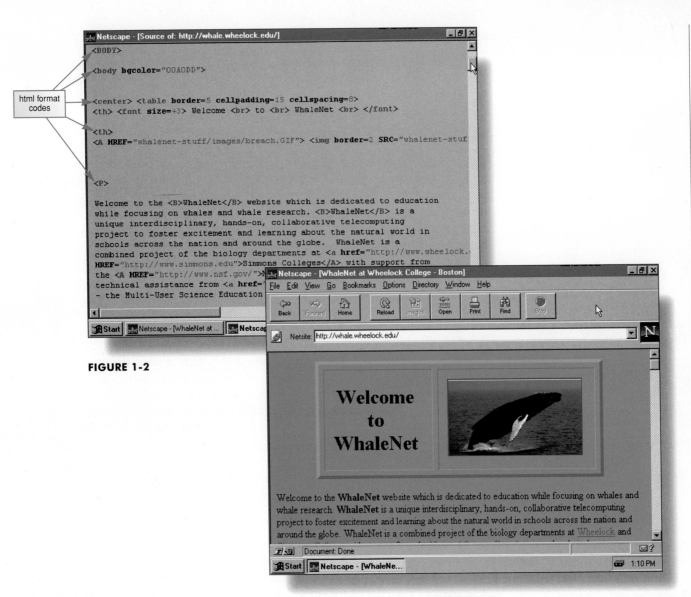

html format
codes

FIGURE 1-2

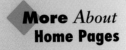

FIGURE 1-3

Home Pages

No main menus or any particular starting points exist in the World Wide Web. Although you can reference any resource on the Internet when you begin, most people start with specially designated pages called **home pages**. A home page is the first page for a Web site, organization, or an individual. All other Web pages for that site, organization, or individual usually can be reached through the home page. In addition, the home page is the default page that displays on your computer if you do not know the address of any other pages located at a particular Web site. Your school may allow you space to create your own home page and publish it on the World Wide Web.

Because it is the starting point for most Web sites, the sites try to make a good first impression and create an attractive home page, with eye-catching graphics, specially formatted text, and a variety of hypertext links to hypermedia contained both at the Web site and at other interesting and useful Web sites.

◆ **More** *About*
Home Pages

A Web site may consist of many home pages. A computer used by faculty members or students for their hypertext documents would have many home pages, one for each person.

Internet Browsers

Just as graphical user interfaces (GUIs) such as Microsoft Windows 95 make using a computer easier by employing a point-and-click method, **browsers** such as Netscape Navigator (Netscape for short) make using the World Wide Web easier by removing the complexity of having to remember the syntax of commands to reference Web pages at Web sites. Today, many browsers are available from different sources.

Mosaic, the first Internet browser, ignited the rise in popularity of the World Wide Web. Netscape, from Netscape Communications Corporation, was developed by some of the same people who wrote Mosaic, keeping the best parts of Mosaic and adding new, user-friendly features. Today, Netscape Navigator is the most popular browser in use, with more than 80% of Web participants using Netscape.

Mouse Usage

In this book, the mouse is used as the primary way to communicate with Netscape Navigator. You can perform six operations with a mouse: point, click, right-click, double-click, drag, and right-drag

Point means you move the mouse across a flat surface until the mouse pointer rests on the item of choice on the screen. As you move the mouse, the mouse pointer moves across the screen in the same direction. **Click** means you press and release the left mouse button. The terminology used in this book to direct you to point to a particular item and then click is, Click the particular item. For example, Click the Home button, means point to the Home button and then click.

Right-click means you press and release the right mouse button. As with the left mouse button, you normally will point to an item on the screen prior to right-clicking.

Double-click means you quickly press and release the left mouse button twice without moving the mouse. In most cases, you must point to an item before double-clicking. **Drag** means you point to an item, hold down the left mouse button, move the item to the desired location on the screen, and then release the left mouse button. **Right-drag** means you point to an item, hold down the right mouse button, move the item to the desired location, and then release the right mouse button.

The use of the mouse is an important skill when working with Netscape Navigator.

Starting Netscape

To start Netscape, the Windows 95 desktop must be on the screen, and the Netscape Navigator shortcut icon must be on the desktop. The Netscape Navigator shortcut icon is created when you install Netscape. Perform the following steps to start Netscape.

More *About* the Mouse

The mouse unit has been around as long as the personal computer itself. However, it had little use with earlier operating systems, such as MS-DOS. Few used the mouse or even attached it to their computer until recently when Windows began to dominate the market. Even with Windows 95, some former MS-DOS users prefer to use the keyboard over the mouse.

Steps **To Start Netscape**

1 **Point to Netscape Navigator shortcut icon on the desktop (Figure 1-4).**

The icons on the Windows 95 desktop may be different on your computer.

Netscape Navigator shortcut icon

mouse pointer

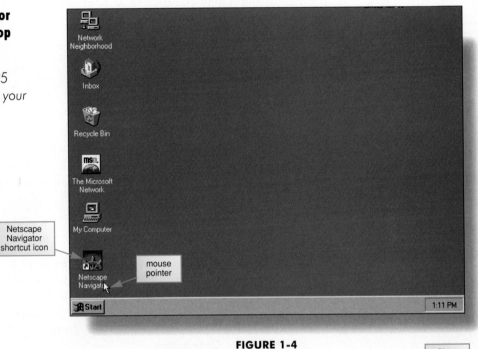

FIGURE 1-4

Close button

title bar

menu bar

2 **Double-click the Netscape Navigator shortcut icon.**

toolbar

The Welcome to Netscape home page displays, indicating you have connected to Netscape Communications Corporation's computer Web site (Figure 1-5). The appearance of this page may display differently on your computer. Netscape Communications Corporation changes its home page often by adding announcements and other interesting elements that provide continuous updates and information.

location text box

directory buttons

display area

taskbar

status indicator

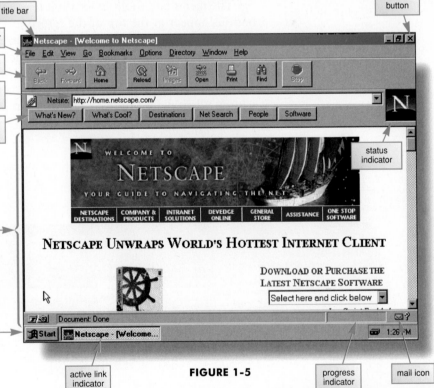

active link indicator

FIGURE 1-5

progress indicator

mail icon

OtherWays

1. Click Start button on taskbar, point to Programs, click Netscape Navigator 3.0, click Netscape Navigator

Normally, when Netscape starts, your computer is connected to a computer at Netscape Communications Corporation, displaying the Netscape home page. It is possible to change the page that displays when Netscape starts. The initial page that displays may be different at your computer center. Some schools have their own home page display when starting Netscape. The name of the home page is displayed in the **title bar** at the top of the screen.

The Netscape Window

The Netscape window (Figure 1-5 on the previous page) consists of features to make browsing the Internet easy. It contains a title bar, menu bar, toolbar, location text box, status indicator, directory buttons, scroll bars, scroll box, scroll arrows, a progress indicator, and a display area where pages from the World Wide Web display.

Display Area

With most pages, only a portion of the page is visible on your screen. You will view the portion of the page displayed on the screen in the **display area**. To the right and at the bottom of the display area are scroll bars, scroll arrows, and a scroll box, which you can use to move the display area up and down or left and right to reveal other parts of the page. In the upper right corner of the window's title bar is the **Close Button**.

The menu bar, toolbar, location text box, status indicator, and directory buttons appear at the top of the screen just below the title bar. The progress indicator appears at the bottom of the screen.

If you scroll down the Netscape home page, you will see underlined blue words. The blue color and underlining identify those phrases as **hypertext links**. Clicking a hypertext link retrieves the linked Web page and displays it on your screen. When placed over a hypertext link, the mouse pointer changes to a pointing hand.

More *About* **the Display Area**

To turn off the display of the starting Web page, use the Appearance sheet in the General Preferences command on the Options menu.

Menu Bar

The **menu bar** displays Netscape menu names (Figure 1-6). Each menu name represents a menu of commands that you can use to perform actions such as saving Web pages on a floppy disk, sending mail, managing bookmarks, setting Netscape options, and accessing frequently used Internet services. To display a menu, such as the File menu in Figure 1-6, click File on the menu bar. To perform an action, on the File menu, click the command name.

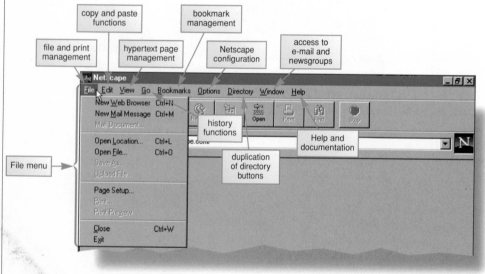

FIGURE 1-6

Toolbar and Directory Buttons

The **toolbar** and **directory buttons** allow you to perform frequent tasks more quickly than when using the menu bar. For example, to print the page being displayed, click the Print button on the toolbar.

Each button on the toolbar contains a word and an icon describing its function. Figures 1-7 and 1-8 illustrate the toolbar and directory buttons and briefly describe the functions of the buttons. Each of the buttons will be explained in detail as it is used.

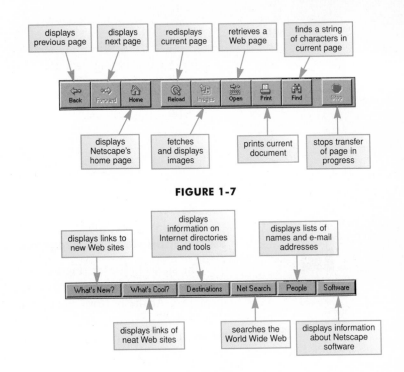

FIGURE 1-7

FIGURE 1-8

Uniform Resource Locator (URL)

Each Web page is identified by a special address called the Uniform Resource Locator. A **Uniform Resource Locator,** or **URL** (pronounced *you are ell*), is important because it is the unique address of each Web page at the Web sites on the World Wide Web.

A typical URL is composed of three parts (Figure 1-9). The first is the protocol. A **protocol** is a set of rules computers follow. Most Web pages use HTTP. **HTTP** stands for **H**yper**T**ext **T**ransport **P**rotocol. HTTP describes the rules for transmitting hypermedia documents electronically. The protocol is entered in lowercase as http, and is followed by a colon and two slashes. Other protocols used on the Web are ftp and gopher.

The second part is the domain name. The **domain name** is the Internet address of the computer on the Internet where the Web page is located. The domain name includes periods and is followed by one slash.

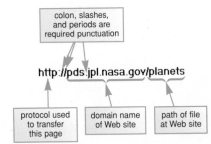

FIGURE 1-9

The third, optional part is the file specification of the Web page. The **file specification** includes the filename and possibly a folder name. This information is called the **path**. If no file specification of a Web page is specified in the URL, a default Web page, usually the Web site's home page, is displayed.

URLs that point to interesting Web pages can be found in magazines, newspapers, browsing the Web, or from friends. Because of the variety and number of URLs, you may find it useful to keep a permanent list of URLs. Netscape has facilities for saving and organizing your favorite URLs so you can access them easily. Later in this project, you will save and retrieve URLs.

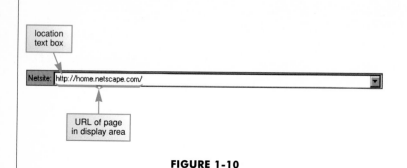

FIGURE 1-10

Location Text Box

The **location text box** (Figure 1-10) contains the Uniform Resource Locator for the page currently shown in the display area of Netscape. It will be updated automatically as you browse from page to page over the World Wide Web. You also can indicate a Web site to connect to by dragging over the current URL in the text box, typing a valid URL, and pressing the ENTER key.

Status Indicator and Progress Indicator

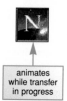

FIGURE 1-11

The **status indicator** (Figure 1-11) goes into motion, or *animates,* while a connection to a Web site is being made and while a page is being retrieved and displayed. At the bottom right of the Netscape window, is a **progress indicator** (Figure 1-12). Acting much like a gauge, it indicates graphically how much of the accessed page has been received from the Web site.

Active Link Indicator

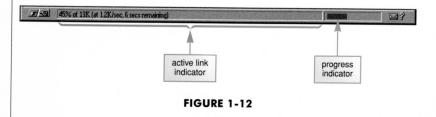

FIGURE 1-12

If the mouse pointer is positioned over an object that has been linked to a Web page, the **active link indicator** displays the URL that will be used to retrieve the page. In addition, if a Web page is being received, the active link indicator provides information about the progress of the transfer of the page (Figure 1-12).

Browsing the World Wide Web

The Welcome To Netscape page (see Figure 1-5 on page NN 1.11) provides a starting point for browsing the World Wide Web. Some of the more interesting and newer pages can be reached by taking advantage of the directory buttons, What's New! and What's Cool! If you click the What's New! button, Netscape displays the What's New! page with links to some of the newer Web pages. If you click the What's Cool! button, Netscape displays the What's Cool! page with links to some of the neatest Web pages.

Netscape Communications Corporation updates the What's New! and What's Cool! pages often as new and extraordinary Web pages become available, so links that appear one day may be gone the next, having been replaced with new offerings.

Two other buttons on the Welcome to Netscape page that allow you to browse the World Wide Web are the directory buttons, Net Search and Destinations. These two buttons allow you to search for topics in which you may be interested. Both buttons will be discussed in detail in Project 2.

The most common way to browse the World Wide Web is to obtain the URL of a Web page you want to visit and enter it into the location text box. Appendix A lists the URLs of some of the more frequently visited Web pages. Practice using Netscape by visiting some of those listed. It is by visiting various Web sites that you can begin to understand the enormous appeal of the World Wide Web. The following steps show you how to contact a Web site provided by NASA, the National Aeronautics and Space Administration, and visit the Web page titled Welcome to the Planets, which contains information and pictures of the planets that make up earth's solar system. The URL for the Welcome to the Planets page is http://pds.jpl.nasa.gov/planets

Steps To Browse the World Wide Web by Entering a URL

1 Click the location text box.

The current URL is high-lighted in the location text box (Figure 1-13).

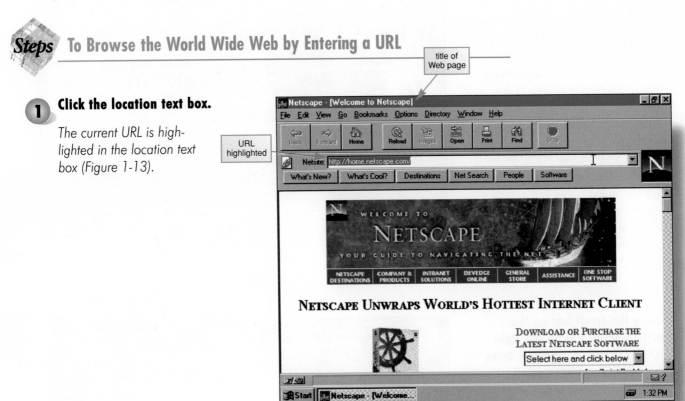

FIGURE 1-13

2 Type http://pds.jpl. nasa.gov/planets **in the location text box.**

The new URL displays in the location text box (Figure 1-14). If you type the wrong letter or symbol in the location text box and notice the error before you move on to the next step, use the BACKSPACE key to erase all the characters back to and including the one that is wrong and then continue typing.

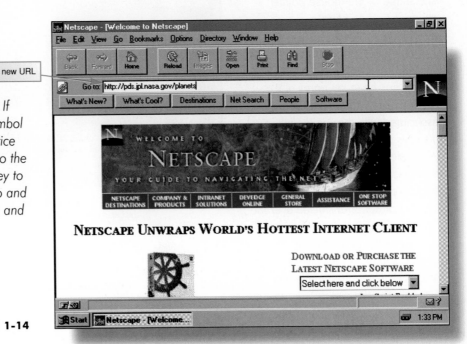

FIGURE 1-14

3 Press the ENTER key.

Netscape begins the transfer of the Welcome to the Planets page from the Web site to your computer. The gray icon in the Stop button on the toolbar changes to red. A message displays in the active link indicator at the bottom of the screen and the progress indicator moves to the right, both providing information about the progress of the transfer. The page starts to display in the display area (Figure 1-15). When the transfer is complete, a message displays in the active link indicator indicating the transfer is complete. The Stop button icon returns to gray and the status indicator motion stops.

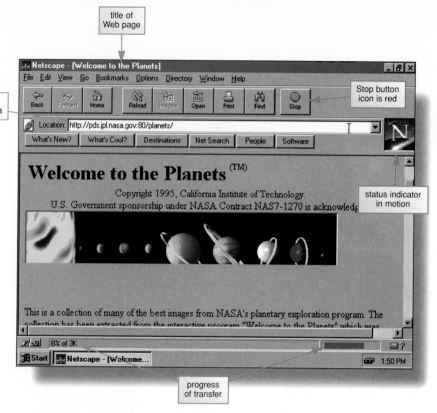

FIGURE 1-15

4 Using the scroll box on the vertical scroll bar on the right side of the window, scroll down the window until the small picture of Jupiter displays. Position the mouse pointer anywhere over the picture.

*The shape of the mouse pointer changes to a pointing hand (Figure 1-16). This change, along with the blue outline, indicates the picture has been set up as a hypertext link. Notice the URL associated with the Jupiter link displays in the active link indicator. It is customary to use small pictures to represent larger pictures or other large Web resources to reduce the amount of data transmitted over the Internet. These small pictures are called **thumbnail** pictures. If you want to see the larger picture or resource behind the thumbnail picture, click the picture.*

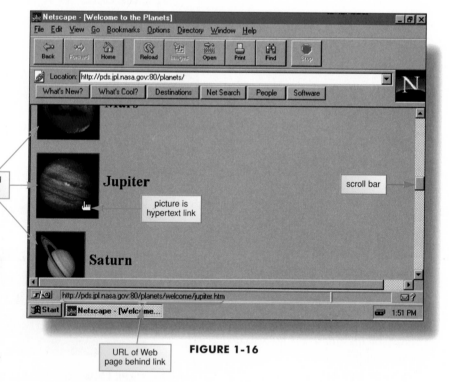

FIGURE 1-16

5 **Click the Jupiter link.**

The Jupiter page starts to display in the display area (Figure 1-17). The gray icon in the Stop button on the toolbar changes to red, the status indicator starts into motion, a message displays at the bottom of the screen, and the progress indicator moves to the right, both providing information about the progress of the transfer. The page is larger than the display area, so you will have to scroll down to reveal the information and pictures that are available for you to see.

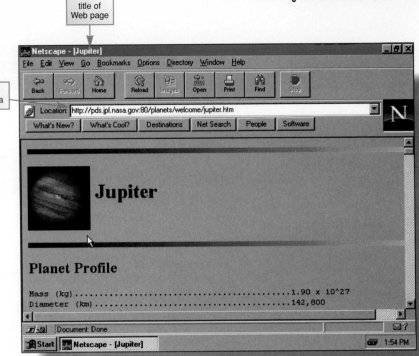

FIGURE 1-17

6 **Scroll down until the thumbnail picture of the White Cloud displays. Position the mouse pointer on the thumbnail picture.**

The mouse pointer changes to a pointing hand (Figure 1-18). A URL displays in the active link indicator. This picture has been set up as a hypertext link.

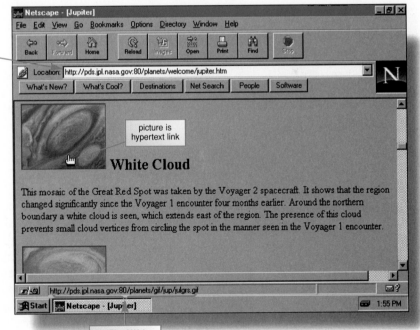

FIGURE 1-18

7 **Click the picture to see a larger image of the White Cloud.**

A large image of the White Cloud starts to display (Figure 1-19).

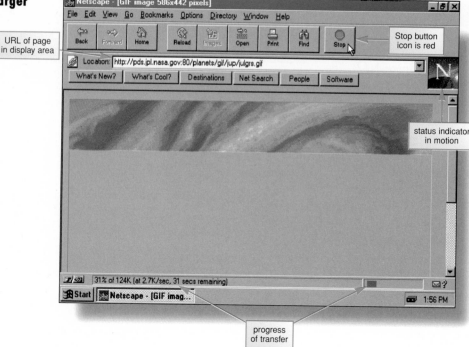

FIGURE 1-19

Other Ways

1. On File menu click Open Location, enter URL in text box, click Open button
2. Press CTRL+L
3. Click Open button on toolbar

More *About* **Thumbnail Pictures**

Some Web page authors will note the size of the resource behind a thumbnail picture to assist in your decision whether or not to retrieve the resource. If an image is several million bytes in size, you might decide not to select the link because it would take too long to transfer to your computer.

You can see from the preceding steps how simple it is to browse the World Wide Web. Traversing hypertext links is as easy as clicking the mouse button. Notice also that hypertext links can be words or pictures. The links can be readily identified by either the blue color and underlining or by the mouse pointer changing to a pointing hand.

Stopping the Transfer of a Page

Some pages are very large and will take time to transfer. After seeing the first portions of a page, you may decide not to wait for the page to finish transferring. You might decide you clicked the wrong hypertext link. Using the **Stop button** on the toolbar, you can stop the ongoing transfer of a page. Recall that while a transfer is in progress, the Stop button icon on the toolbar is the color red. You can stop a transfer only while it is in progress. That means if the Stop button icon no longer is red (returns to gray), the page has been completely received. Therefore, you cannot stop the transfer. Because the White Cloud picture is fairly large, it could take 20 to 30 seconds to arrive. The following step shows how to interrupt the transfer. Remember, this step will work only if the Stop button icon is still red.

Steps To Stop a Page in Transfer

1 **Click the Stop button on the toolbar displaying the red icon.**

The Stop button icon changes to gray, and the status indicator motion stops. Any portions of the page that have arrived will display (Figure 1-20).

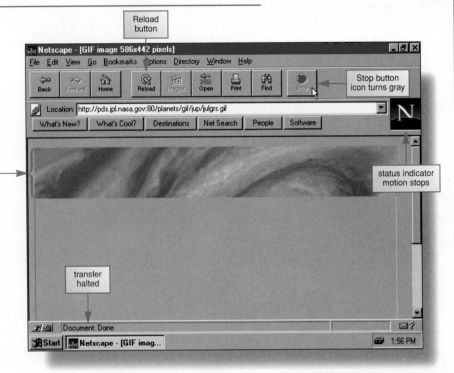

FIGURE 1-20

Stopping the loading of a document will leave a partially loaded Web page. Any pictures or text that arrived before the transfer was halted can be viewed, and any hypertext links that arrived can be clicked to follow those links.

Reloading Pages

If you decide you want the complete page transferred, you can reload the page using the **Reload button**, as shown in the step on the next page.

*Other***Ways**

1. On Go menu click Stop Loading
2. Press ESC

More *About* **Loading Pages**

You can speed up the display of a Web page by unchecking the Auto Load Images on the Options menu. When this menu item is unchecked, the images in pages are replaced by small icons. To manually load an individual image, click on the image's icon.

Steps **To Reload a Page**

1 **Click the Reload button on the toolbar.**

The picture of the White Cloud displays (Figure 1-21). This type of picture is a GIF image. **GIF***, which stands for* **G***raphics* **I***nterchange* **F***ormat, is a technique for encoding pictures on computers. The numbers 586x442 indicate the number of pixels, or picture elements, that make up the image. A* **pixel** *is the smallest addressable point on the CRT screen.*

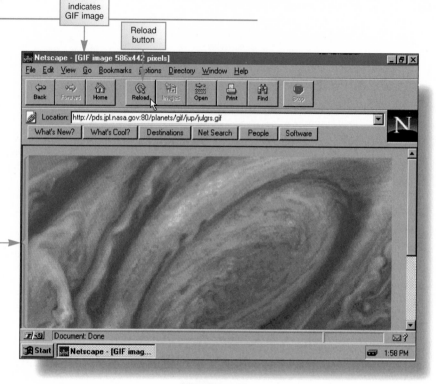

FIGURE 1-21

Other*Ways*
1. On View menu click Reload
2. Press CTRL+R

If the connection to the Web site where the page is located becomes broken and the page transfer does not finish, you can use the Reload button to request the page again.

Another way to request a page is by clicking in the location text box. The URL becomes highlighted. By pressing the ENTER key, you will request the page indicated by the URL, or you can type a new URL, requesting a new page to be displayed. Using the steps and techniques just presented, you have learned how to follow hypertext links and browse the World Wide Web.

History List

As you display different Web pages, Netscape keeps track of the ones you visit in a special area called a **history list**. The history list starts out empty every time you start Netscape. The URLs of the pages you display, in the order you visit them, then are stored in the history list by Netscape. You can determine quickly if URLs are stored in the history list by looking at the **Back button** or the **Forward button** on the toolbar. When Netscape first starts, both buttons are gray, or **ghosted**, which means they are inactive. As you follow links, the Back button icon changes to the color blue. This lets you know that the button is active and URLs of pages you have displayed are stored in the history list.

By using the Back and Forward buttons on the toolbar, you can travel back and forth quickly through the history list redisplaying the pages you have visited. Perform the following steps to move through the history list.

Steps To Move Back and Forth in the History List

title of page
in display area

1 Click the Back button on the toolbar.

The middle of the page titled Jupiter redisplays (Figure 1-22). The Forward button icon changes from gray to blue. This indicates the page displayed is somewhere in the middle of the history list, with URLs behind and in front of the URL of the page currently in the display area. Notice that the border around the thumbnail picture is no longer is blue. It has changed to pink. This is an indication that the link has been visited previously.

Back and Forward buttons active

pink color indicates this page recently visited

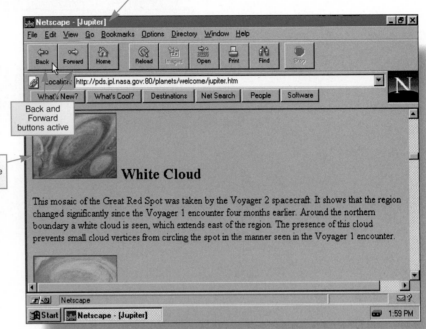

FIGURE 1-22

title of page
in display area

2 Click the Back button on the toolbar again.

The middle of the page titled Welcome to the Planets redisplays (Figure 1-23). You can continue to page backward until you reach the beginning of the history list. At that time, the Back button icon changes color from blue to gray, indicating that no additional pages to which you can move back are contained in the history list. You can move forward by clicking the Forward button.

Back button

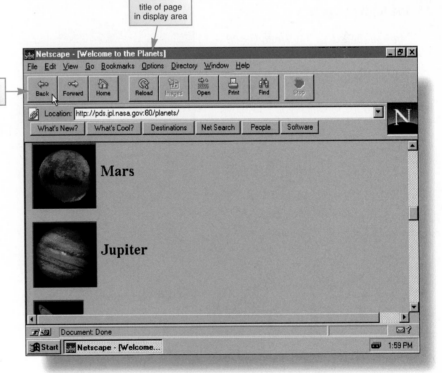

FIGURE 1-23

3 Click the Forward button on the toolbar.

The middle of the page titled Jupiter redisplays (Figure 1-24).

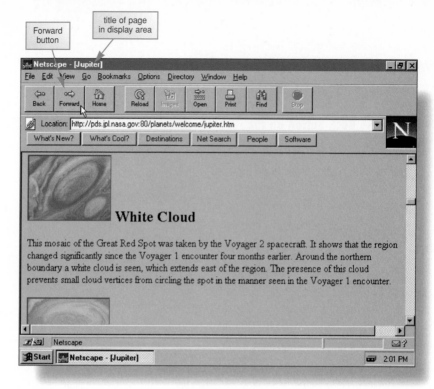

FIGURE 1-24

4 Click the Forward button on the toolbar again.

The GIF image of the White Cloud redisplays (Figure 1-25). Notice the Forward button icon changes from blue to gray indicating no additional pages to which you can move forward.

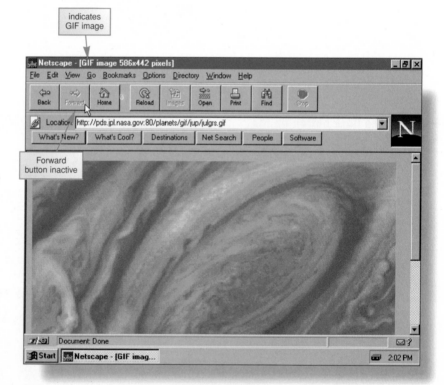

FIGURE 1-25

OtherWays

1. On Go menu click Back to move back or click Forward to move forward
2. Press ALT+LEFT ARROW to move back or ALT+RIGHT ARROW to move forward

You can see that traversing through the history list is easy using the toolbar buttons. Notice each page is redisplayed as you click the Back or Forward button. With many pages to display before the one you want, it could take a while to get to it. It is possible to skip around in the history list without redisplaying any intermediate pages.

Displaying a Web Page Using the History List

Using the history list, you can return directly to any of the pages you have visited. First, display the entire history list, and then click the line containing the page title, as shown in the following steps.

 Steps To Display a Web Page Using the History List

1 Click Go on the menu bar.

The Go menu displays (Figure 1-26). The titles of the pages you have visited display in the history list with a check mark next to the currently displayed page. The URLs are numbered with the oldest page having the highest number.

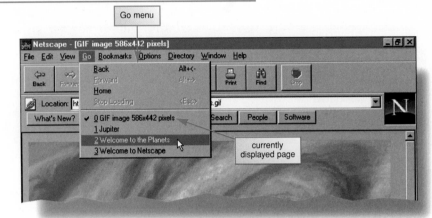

FIGURE 1-26

2 Click Welcome to the Planets in the history list, the entry labeled number 2.

The middle of the page titled Welcome to the Planets redisplays (Figure 1-27). The Forward button icon turns blue, indicating there are pages to which you can move forward.

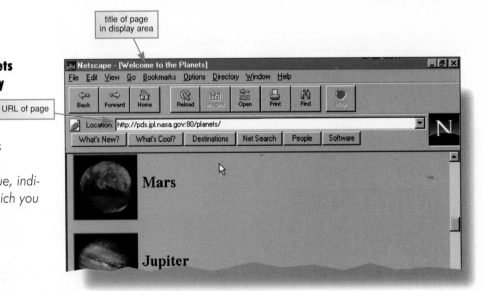

FIGURE 1-27

If you have a small history list or the page you want is only one or two pages away, it is much quicker to use the Back and Forward buttons on the toolbar to traverse the history list than to bring up the history list and select pages. If you have visited a large number of Web pages, however, your history list will be long, and it might be easier to use the history list to select the exact page to redisplay. Remember, using the Back and Forward buttons on the toolbar causes intermediate pages to be redisplayed.

History lists are useful for returning to a Web page you have recently visited. Unfortunately, you cannot use the history list to permanently store the URLs of your favorite, or frequently-visited, pages. Recall that the history list starts out empty each time you start Netscape.

More *About* **Redisplaying Web Pages**

Displayed Web pages are stored in a special area on disk called a cache. That way, if the Web page is requested again, it can be displayed from the cache much faster than having to contact the remote Web site and then be transferred over the Internet again.

You can see from the previous figures that URLs can be long and cryptic (Figure 1-25 on page NN 1.22). It would be easy to make a mistake while writing down such long, cryptic addresses. Fortunately, Netscape has capabilities for keeping track of your favorite Web pages. You can permanently store the URLs of your favorite pages in an area called a **bookmark list**.

Keeping Track of Your Favorite Web Pages

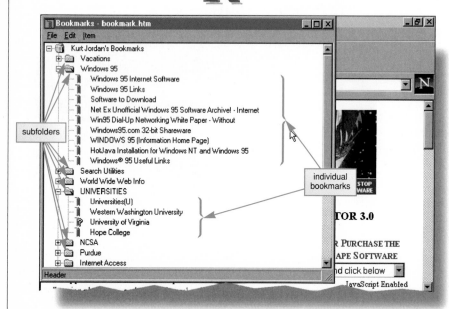

FIGURE 1-28

The bookmark feature of Netscape allows you to save the URLs of your favorite Web pages. A **bookmark** consists of the title of the Web page and the URL of that page. Think of the bookmark list as an electronic address book containing the URL and page title of Web pages that are important to you. You can add new bookmarks and remove bookmarks you no longer want. Figure 1-28 shows a well-organized bookmark list, with sets of bookmarks organized under appropriate headings. The following steps show how to add the Welcome to the Planets URL to the bookmark list.

Steps To Add a Bookmark to the Bookmark List

1 **Click Bookmarks on the menu bar.**

The Bookmarks menu displays (Figure 1-29). The two commands are Add Bookmark, which adds the current URL to the book-mark list and Go to Bookmarks, which displays bookmark details. The title portion of any existing bookmarks would appear on the menu below the Go to Bookmarks command. If this is your first time using Netscape, probably no bookmarks will be listed, as is the case in Figure 1-29.

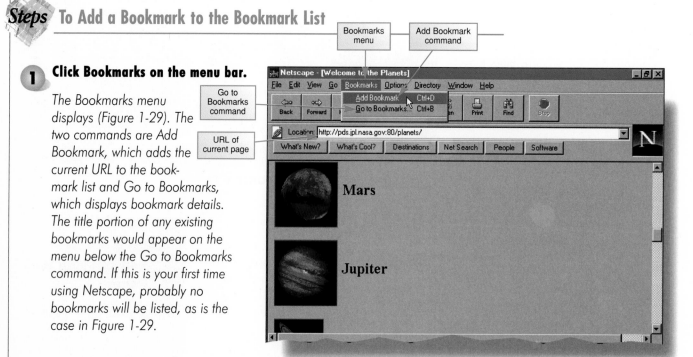

FIGURE 1-29

2 **Click Add Bookmark.**

The Bookmarks menu disappears. The title of the current page in the display area is added to the end of the bookmark list.

3 **Click Bookmarks on the menu bar to verify the page has been added to the bookmark list.**

The Bookmarks menu displays, containing the newly added bookmark (Figure 1-30). You may see other bookmarks already added. The bookmark you added should be the last one in the list.

4 **Close the Bookmarks menu by clicking Bookmarks on the menu bar. Click the Home button on the toolbar to redisplay the Netscape home page.**

The Bookmarks menu disappears and the Netscape home page displays as shown in Figure 1-5 on page NN 1.11. The Netscape home page was redisplayed to demonstrate recalling a Web page using a bookmark.

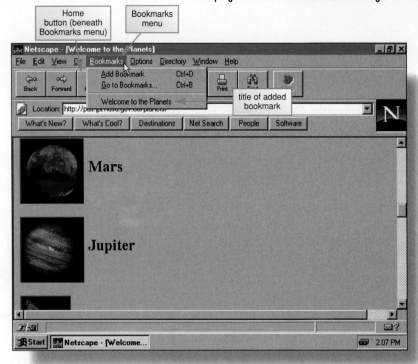

FIGURE 1-30

Other bookmarks you add will be listed below Welcome to the Planets. The size of the Bookmarks menu will grow as you add new bookmarks.

Retrieving a Web Page Using a Bookmark

Bookmarks can be used to quickly display favorite or frequently accessed Web pages without having to navigate through several unwanted pages. Using a bookmark to display a Web page is similar to using the history list to display a Web page. To retrieve the Web page pointed to by the URL associated with the bookmark, perform the steps on the next page.

Other*Ways*

1. Press CTRL+D
2. Press ALT+B, press letter A

More *About*
Bookmark Titles

The title that identifies a bookmark can be changed by displaying the bookmarks, highlighting the bookmark entry and clicking Properties on the Item menu. Then, key in a new title and click OK.

Steps To Retrieve a Web Page Using a Bookmark

1 **Click Bookmarks on the menu bar.**

The Bookmarks menu displays (Figure 1-31). The list of available bookmarks appears below the Go to Bookmarks command. The Welcome to the Planets bookmark should be the last bookmark on the list.

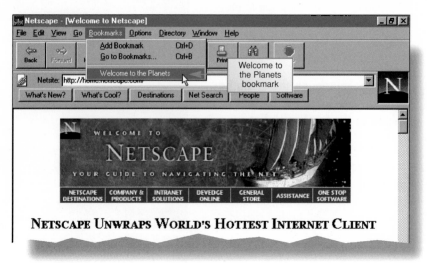

FIGURE 1-31

2 **Click Welcome to the Planets.**

The Welcome to the Planets page redisplays (Figure 1-32).

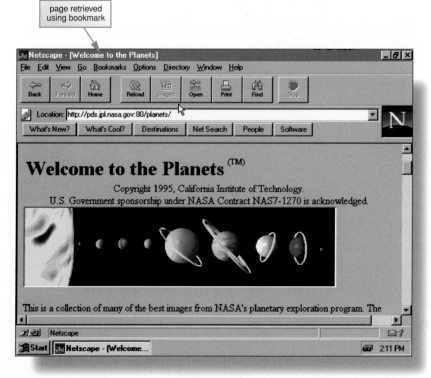

FIGURE 1-32

You have learned how to add a URL to the bookmark list and how to retrieve that resource using the bookmark list. Your bookmark list will become an important asset, growing as you add new entries while exploring the World Wide Web. To protect your bookmark list, it is a good idea to save it on a floppy disk.

Saving Your Bookmark List

If you are using Netscape in an environment where several individuals are using the same computer — for example, in a college computer lab — you need the capability to save your bookmarks so you can carry them with you and reuse them in Netscape. Restoring your bookmarks will be shown later in this project. The following steps show how to save your bookmark list to a floppy disk.

 Steps **To Save a Bookmark List to a Floppy Disk**

1 **Insert a floppy disk in drive B.**

The drive designation on your computer may be different.

2 **Click Bookmarks on the menu bar, and then click Go to Bookmarks.**

The Netscape Bookmarks window displays (Figure 1-33). Notice the Welcome to the Planets bookmark you added. Other bookmarks may appear on your computer. The Bookmarks menus contain commands used to manage bookmarks.

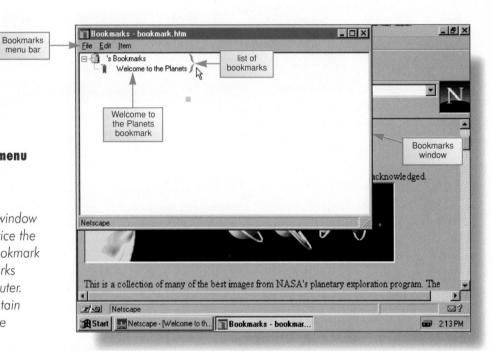

FIGURE 1-33

3 **Click File on the Bookmarks menu bar.**

The File menu displays (Figure 1-34). The Save As command saves the bookmark list to a disk file.

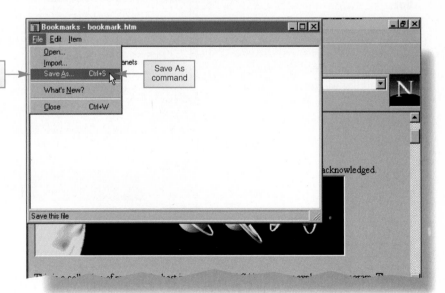

FIGURE 1-34

4 **Click Save As.**

The Save bookmarks file dialog box displays (Figure 1-35). The default folder is Navigator. Save bookmarks file dialog box *The default filename is bookmark. These may be different on your computer, and the default filename may not display in the File name text box.*

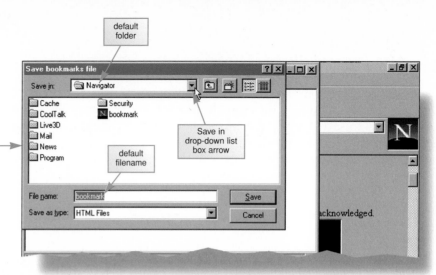

FIGURE 1-35

5 **Type** bookmark **in the File name text box, if necessary. Click the Save in drop-down list box arrow.**

The Save in drop-down list displays a list of various elements of your computer (Figure 1-36). If the 3½ Floppy [B:] icon does not appear in the list, use the up scroll box arrow to bring it into view. The drive designation on your computer may be different.

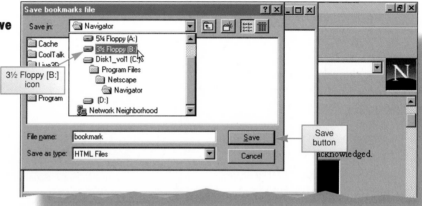

FIGURE 1-36

6 **Click the 3½ Floppy [B:] icon in the Save in drop-down list box.**

The 3½ Floppy [B:] becomes the selected drive (Figure 1-37). The dialog box indicates that the bookmark list will be saved on a floppy disk in drive B in a file named bookmark.

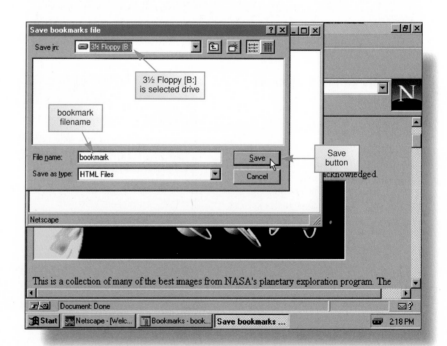

FIGURE 1-37

7 **Click the Save button.**

The Netscape Bookmarks window redisplays (Figure 1-38). The bookmark list has been saved to a floppy disk.

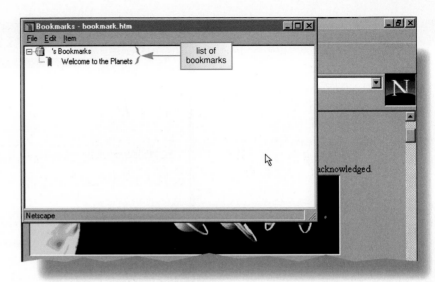

FIGURE 1-38

Other Ways
1. Press CTRL+B
2. Press ALT+F, press letter A

Your bookmark list now is saved on a floppy disk in drive A. With your bookmark list saved on the floppy disk, you can use your bookmarks on any computer running Netscape. As you gain experience and continue to browse the World Wide Web, adding pages to your bookmark list, it is likely a time will come when you will want to remove unwanted bookmarks from the list.

Removing Bookmarks

Several reasons exist for wanting to remove a bookmark. With the World Wide Web changing every day, the URL that worked today might not work tomorrow. Perhaps you just do not want a particular bookmark in your list anymore. The following steps show how to remove a bookmark from the bookmark list.

 To Remove a Bookmark from the Bookmark List

1 **With the Netscape Bookmarks window displayed, click Welcome to the Planets to select that bookmark as the one to be deleted.**

The Welcome to the Planets bookmark is highlighted (Figure 1-39).

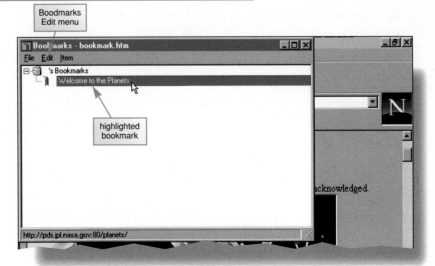

FIGURE 1-39

2 **Click Edit on the Bookmarks menu bar.**

The Edit menu displays (Figure 1-40). The Edit menu contains commands to manage individual or sets of bookmarks. The Delete command removes highlighted bookmarks.

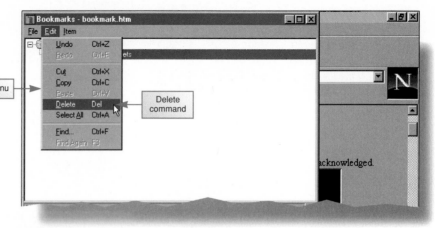

FIGURE 1-40

3 **Click Delete to remove the highlighted bookmark.**

The Welcome to the Planets bookmark disappears (Figure 1-41).

4 **Click the Close button in the Bookmarks window title bar.**

The Netscape Bookmarks window disappears.

5 **To verify that the bookmark has been removed, click Bookmarks on the menu bar.**

The Bookmarks menu displays. The Welcome to the Planets bookmark is removed.

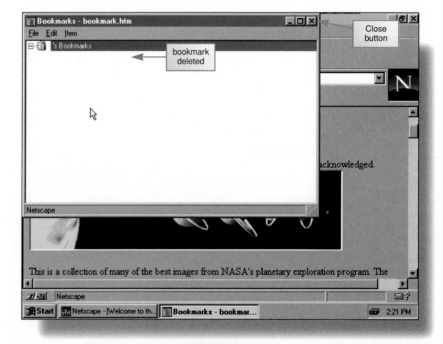

FIGURE 1-41

6 **Click Bookmarks menu to close it.**

The Bookmarks menu disappears.

OtherWays

1. Click bookmark to highlight it, press DELETE

Using the functions in the Netscape Bookmarks window makes it easy to manage your bookmarks. Netscape provides many other advanced features for handling bookmarks. For example, you can create hierarchical menus that allow you to organize your bookmark list into logical categories (see Figure 1-28 on page NN 1.24) or import new bookmarks.

Importing Bookmarks from a Floppy Disk

Even when using Netscape on different computers, such as in a college computer lab, or the library, you probably will want to use your personal bookmark list. This means you have to **import**, or read in, your bookmark list from a floppy disk. The steps for restoring your bookmarks from the floppy disk are much the same as for saving bookmarks.

Steps To Import a Bookmark List from a Floppy Disk

1 **Insert the floppy disk with your bookmarks into drive B.**

The drive may be different on your computer.

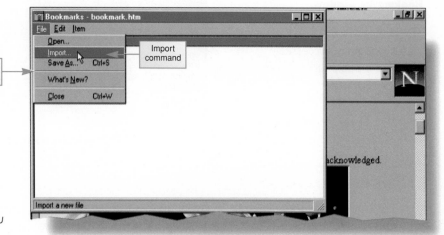

FIGURE 1-42

2 **Click Bookmarks on the menu bar, click Go to Bookmarks, and then click File on the Bookmarks menu bar.**

The Netscape Bookmarks File menu displays (Figure 1-42). The Import command reads bookmarks from a disk file.

3 **Click Import to read in the bookmark file from the floppy disk.**

The Import bookmarks file dialog box displays (Figure 1-43). The 3½ Floppy [B:] should be the current drive, because it was selected earlier when saving your bookmark file. The names of any files on the floppy disk display in the dialog box below the Look in box. The filename, bookmark, is the file you saved in earlier steps. Other files may be present on the floppy disk. The icon next to the bookmark filename identifies it as an html file. The drive may be different on your computer.

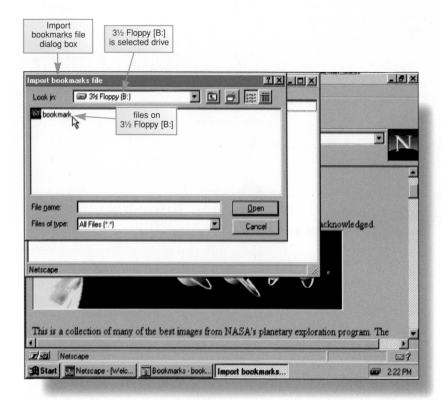

FIGURE 1-43

4 **Click bookmark and then click the Open button.**

The Netscape Bookmarks window displays. The bookmark file is read in from the floppy disk in drive B, and appended to the bottom of the list of bookmarks in the Bookmarks window (Figure 1-44).

5 **Click the Close button in the Bookmarks window.**

The Netscape Bookmarks window closes. You have successfully imported a bookmark list from a floppy disk.

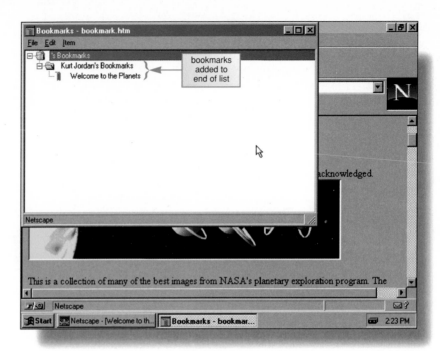

FIGURE 1-44

By saving and importing your bookmark list, you can use your personal collection of bookmarks to access the World Wide Web from any computer on the Internet that is running Netscape. Notice that your bookmarks are added to the bottom of any bookmarks that are already in the bookmark list. That is why the Kurt Jordan's Bookmarks heading appears twice in the Bookmarks window.

You must be careful if you import your bookmarks, make changes, and then want to save the bookmarks back to a floppy disk. You not only will save yours, but other, perhaps unwanted, bookmarks. You should check for and delete any unwanted bookmarks before importing or saving your bookmark list when sharing a computer with several users.

You have learned how to create, use, save to a floppy disk, remove, and import bookmarks. Saving URLs in the bookmark list is not the only way to save information you obtain using Netscape. Some of the more interesting text and pictures you display while connecting to various Web sites also will be worth saving.

Saving Information Obtained with Netscape

Many different types of Web pages are available on the World Wide Web. Because these pages can help you accumulate information about areas of interest, you might want to save the information you discover for future reference. The different types of Web pages and the different ways you may want to use them require different ways of saving them. Netscape can save individual pictures, selected pieces of a Web page, or the entire Web page.

Saving a Web Page

The following steps show how to save the currently displayed Web page to a floppy disk in drive B.

Steps To Save a Web Page

1 **Insert a floppy disk into drive B.**

The drive may be different on your computer.

2 **Click File on the menu bar.**

The File menu displays (Figure 1-45). The File menu contains commands to manage Web pages. The Save As command writes a Web page to a floppy disk file.

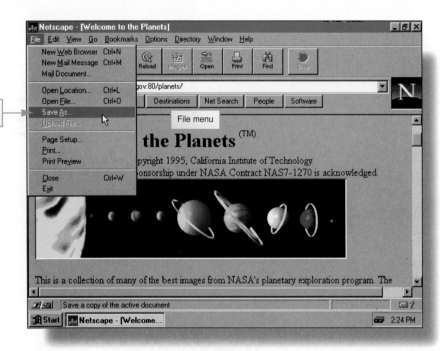

FIGURE 1-45

3 **Click Save As.**

The Save As dialog box displays (Figure 1-46). Drive B still should be the current drive. The filename, planets, is used as the default filename because that is the name of the file containing the Web page at the NASA Web site.

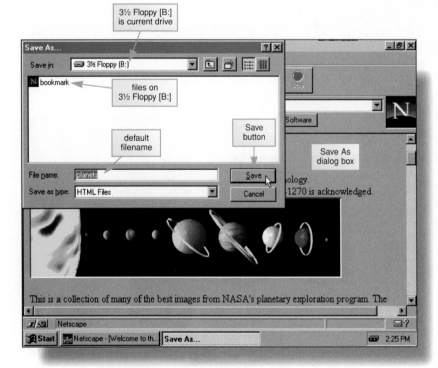

FIGURE 1-46

4 **Click the Save button to accept the filename of planets.**

A Saving Location dialog box displays momentarily, indicating the progress of the save operation (Figure 1-47). When the page has been saved, the dialog box disappears.

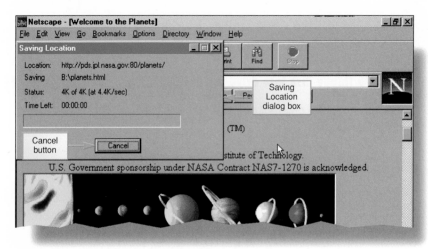

FIGURE 1-47

The document now is stored as a regular disk file and can be opened by any Windows word processor. The saving operation can be canceled by clicking the Cancel button.

Saving a Picture on a Web Page

If you are interested only in the pictures on the page, the following steps illustrate how to save an image from a Web page on a floppy disk in drive B.

Steps To Save a Picture on a Web Page

1 **With the Welcome to the Planets page displayed, right-click anywhere in the picture at the top of the page containing the sun and several planets. Make sure you right-click, because if the picture is set up as a hypertext link, you will cause Netscape to retrieve the Web page for that particular link if you simply click it.**

A shortcut menu displays (Figure 1-48).

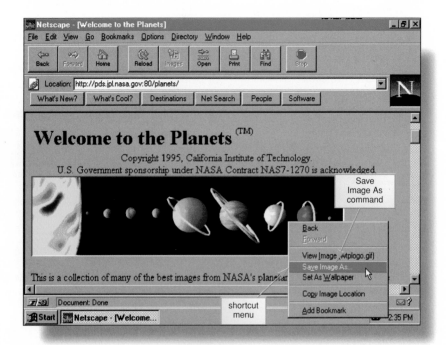

FIGURE 1-48

2 **Click Save Image As on the shortcut menu.**

The Save As dialog box displays (Figure 1-49). Drive B is still the current drive. The default filename is wtplogo.

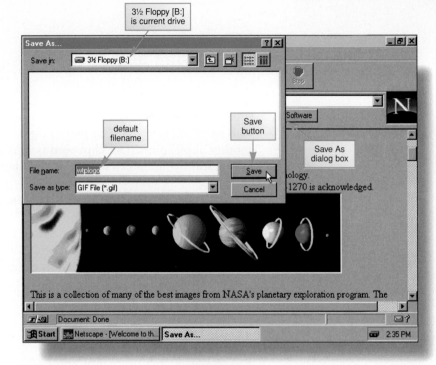

FIGURE 1-49

3 **Click the Save button to save the wtplogo filename.**

The Saving Location dialog box displays, indicating the progress of the save operation (Figure 1-50). When the picture has been saved, the dialog box disappears.

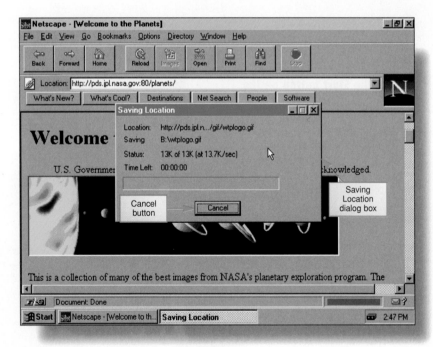

FIGURE 1-50

The picture now is stored as a file on your floppy disk and can be displayed with image viewers such as Paintbrush or a Windows word processor. The last technique for saving information uses the Clipboard to insert portions of a Web page into a Notepad file. **Notepad** is a text editor provided with Microsoft Windows 95.

Copying and Pasting Using the Clipboard

More *About*
About Saving

You can cause an image to become the wallpaper image for Windows by right-clicking the image and then clicking Set as wallpaper.

Portions of, or even an entire Web page can be inserted into another Windows application, such as Notepad, using copy and paste facilities. The portion of the Web page you select will be placed on the Clipboard and then can be inserted into another application. The **Clipboard** is a temporary storage area in main memory. Information you cut or copy to the Clipboard remains there until you change it or clear it.

To begin the operation, you will open Microsoft Notepad using the Start button. Next, you must switch back to Netscape and copy to the Clipboard the portion of the text you want to paste in the Notepad document. Finally, you will switch back to Notepad and paste the contents from the Clipboard into the document. These steps are shown in the following sections.

Starting Notepad

To start Notepad, use the Start button to display the Accessories submenu. Once Notepad is started and the appropriate document is opened, switch to Netscape using the taskbar as shown in the following steps.

Steps **To Start Notepad**

1 **Click the Start button on the taskbar. Point to Programs on the Start menu. Point to Accessories on the Programs submenu, and then point to Notepad on the Accessories submenu.**

The Start menu and Programs and Accessories submenus display (Figure 1-51).

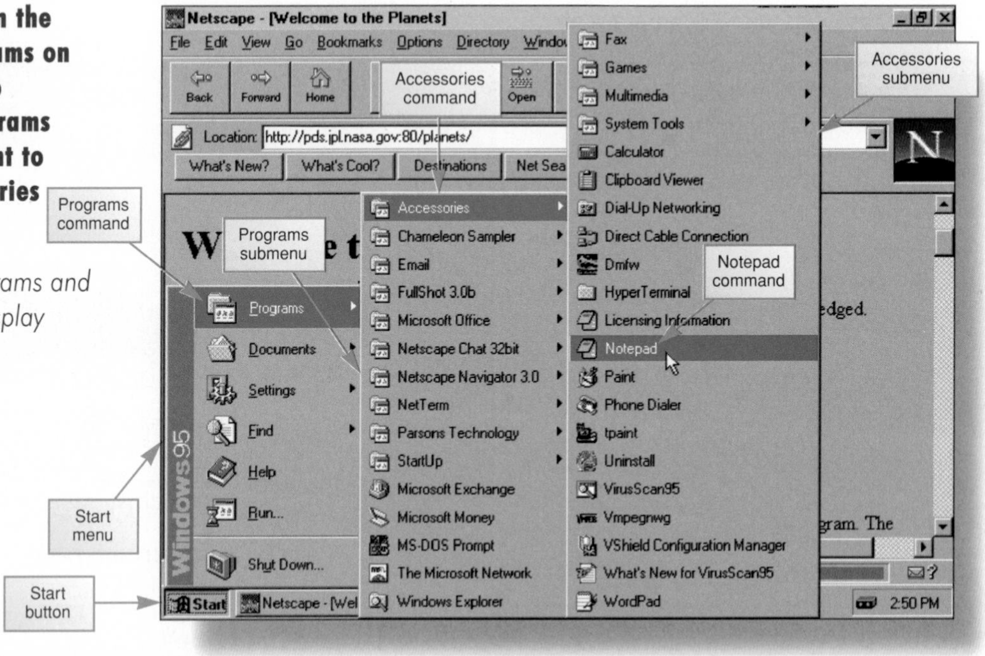

FIGURE 1-51

2 **Click Notepad.**

Windows starts the Notepad application and then the Notepad window displays (Figure 1-52).

3 **Click the Netscape button on the taskbar.**

Netscape Navigator becomes active. The Welcome to the Planets page displays as shown in Figure 1-32 on page NN 1.26.

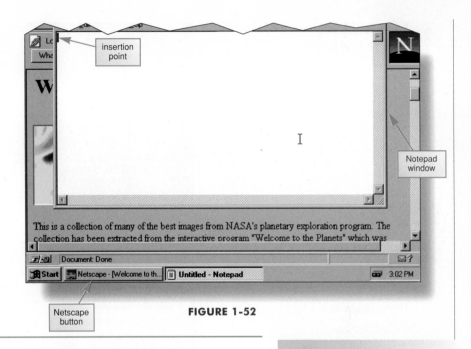

FIGURE 1-52

With the Notepad application started, the next step is to complete the copy and paste operation.

Copying Text from a Web Page and Pasting It in Notepad

The following steps show how to copy planet profile information about the planet Jupiter to the Clipboard, switch to Notepad, and paste the text on the Clipboard into the Notepad document.

More *About* **Copying and Pasting**

Images and pictures on a Web page cannot be copied to the Clipboard by dragging over them. To copy an image to another Windows application, save the image in a disk file, start the other Windows application, and then import or insert the file containing the saved image.

 Steps **To Copy and Paste a Section of a Web Page into Notepad**

1 **Scroll down the Welcome to the Planets page and click the picture of Jupiter. Scroll down the Jupiter page to reveal the Planet Profile information.**

The Planet Profile information displays (Figure 1-53).

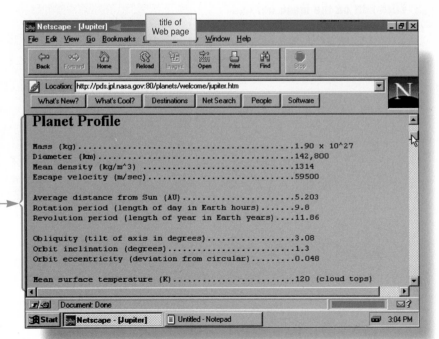

FIGURE 1-53

2 Point to the beginning of the text (Figure 1-54).

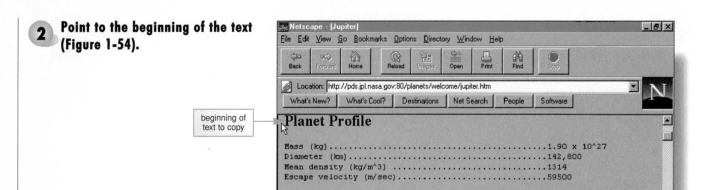

FIGURE 1-54

3 Drag from the beginning of the text to the end of the text to select it.

The selected text is highlighted (Figure 1-55).

FIGURE 1-55

4 Click Edit on the menu bar and then point to Copy.

The Edit menu displays (Figure 1-56).

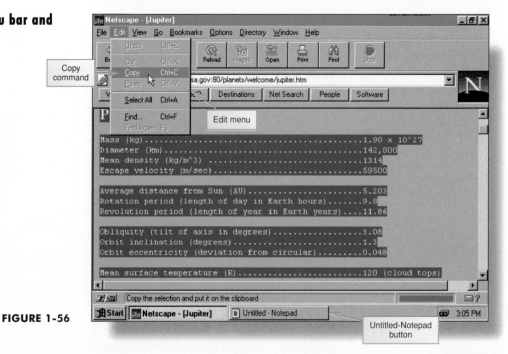

FIGURE 1-56

5 **Click Copy.**

The Edit menu closes and the selected text is copied to the Clipboard.

6 **Click the Untitled - Notepad button on the taskbar.**

Windows 95 displays the Notepad window.

7 **Click Edit on the Notepad menu bar.**

The Edit menu displays (Figure 1-57).

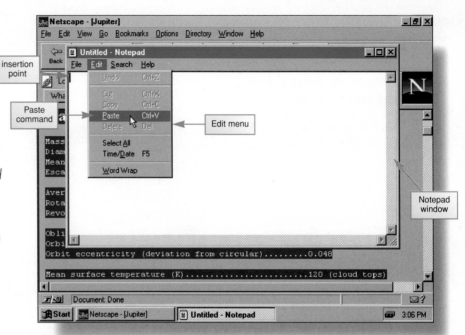

FIGURE 1-57

8 **Click Paste.**

The contents of the Clipboard are pasted in the Notepad window beginning at the location of the insertion point (Figure 1-58).

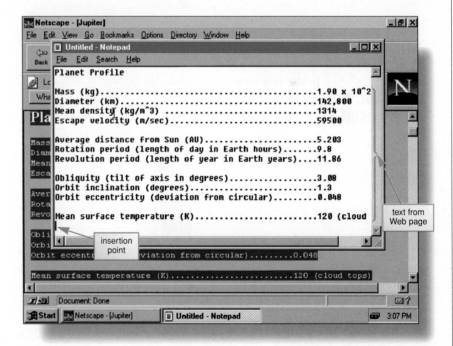

FIGURE 1-58

The copy and paste operation is complete. The Notepad document contains a paragraph of text you retrieved from the World Wide Web. You also can use this technique for inserting the URL in the location text box into another application.

Saving the Notepad Document

When you are finished with the Notepad document, you can save it on a floppy disk and then exit Notepad, as shown in the steps on the next page.

Other Ways

1. Highlight text to be copied, press CTRL+C to copy

2. Position insertion point where text is to appear, press CTRL+V to paste

Steps   To Save the Notepad Document and Exit Notepad

1 Click File on the Notepad menu bar and then click Save As.

The Save As dialog box displays (Figure 1-59). Desktop is the default folder.

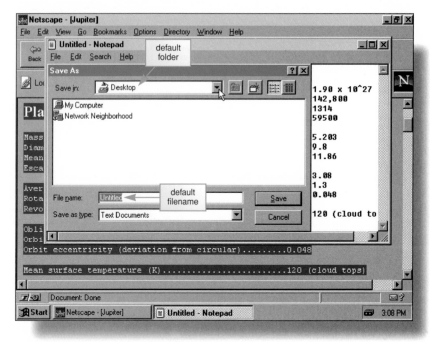

FIGURE 1-59

2 Type Jupiter in the File name text box. Click the Save in box arrow. Click 3½ Floppy [B:].

The filename jupiter replaces the default filename (Untitled) (Figure 1-60). Drive B becomes the current drive.

3 Click the Save button.

The Save As dialog box disappears, and the Notepad file is saved on the floppy disk in drive B.

4 Click the Close button in the Notepad window to close Notepad.

Notepad closes, and the Netscape window redisplays as shown in Figure 1-55 on page NN 1.38.

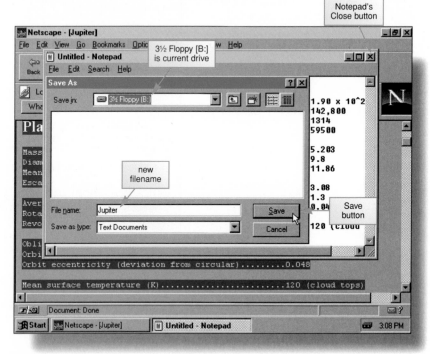

FIGURE 1-60

In the previous steps, you pasted into Notepad. Using the same techniques, you can paste into any Windows application installed on your computer.

You have learned how to save information you retrieve from a Web site. In addition to saving, Netscape allows you to print the pages you find interesting as you travel around the Web.

Printing a Web Page in Netscape

Netscape's printing capabilities allow you to print both the text and graphic portions of a Web page. The easiest way to print is to use the **Print button** on the toolbar. The following steps print the Welcome to the Planets Web page.

More *About* **Printing**

The title and URL of a Web page that appear at the top of a printout can be suppressed using the Page Setup command on the File menu.

 Steps To Print a Web Page

1 **Ready the printer according to the printer instructions. Click the Back button to redisplay the Welcome to the Planets Web page.**

The Welcome to the Planets Web page displays.

2 **Click the Print button on the toolbar.**

The Print dialog box displays (Figure 1-61). All is selected in the Print range area, indicating the entire document will print, regardless of its length.

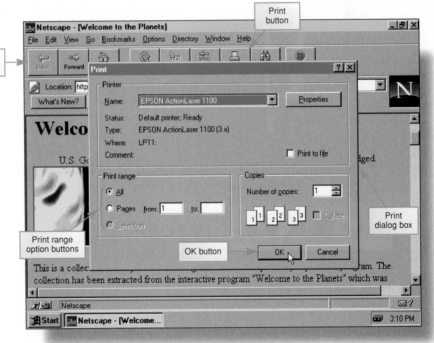

FIGURE 1-61

3 **Click the OK button to print the entire Web page.**

The Printing Status dialog box displays indicating the printing status (Figure 1-62). When the document has been sent to the printer, the dialog box disappears, returning control to the Netscape window. If, for any reason, you wish to cancel the print operation, click the Cancel button.

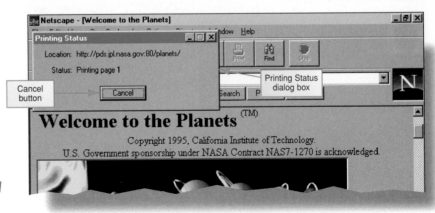

FIGURE 1-62

5 **When the printer stops, retrieve the printout (Figure 1-63).**

Notice the title and URL of the Web page appear on the printout.

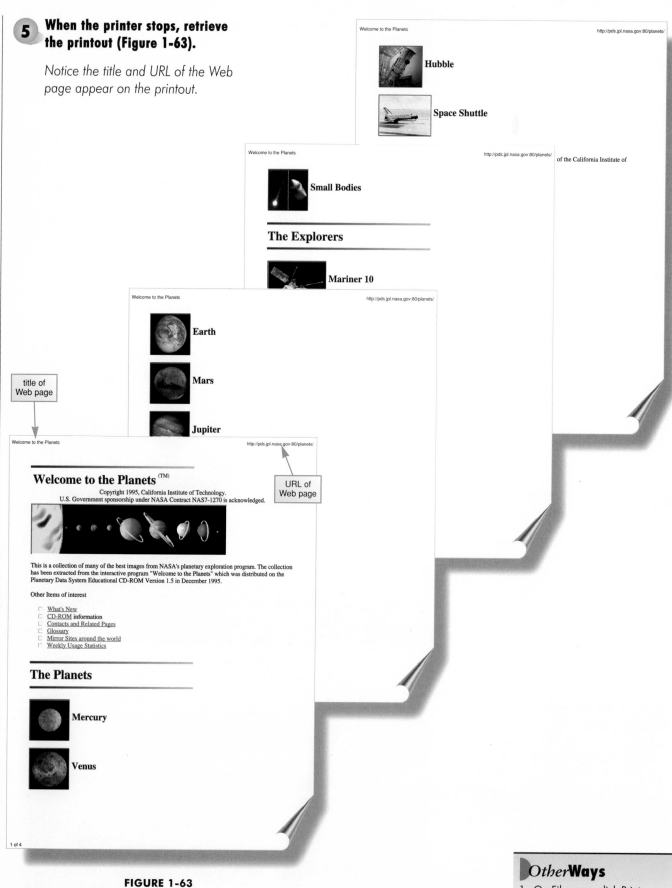

title of Web page

URL of Web page

FIGURE 1-63

OtherWays

1. On File menu click Print
2. Press ALT+F, press letter P

Notice the printing options in the Print dialog box in Figure 1-61 on page NN 1.41. You can print the entire document or selected pages of the document. The document can be printed to a disk file. Multiple copies of what you print can be selected. Printer properties can be changed, and the printing request can be canceled, returning you to the Netscape window. The Cancel button in the Netscape dialog box (Figure 1-62 on page NN 1.41) allows you to cancel the print request.

Netscape Online Help

Netscape is a program with many features and options. Although you will master some of these features and options quickly, it is not necessary for you to remember everything about each one of them.

Reference materials and other forms of assistance are available from within Netscape. You can retrieve these materials and use the methods previously discussed to print or save them on a floppy disk. The following steps show how to obtain information about saving to a hard disk.

Steps **To Access Help in Netscape**

1 **Click Help on the menu bar and then point to Handbook.**

The Help menu displays (Figure 1-64). Several commands are available to display information about Netscape. The Handbook command contains information on using Netscape.

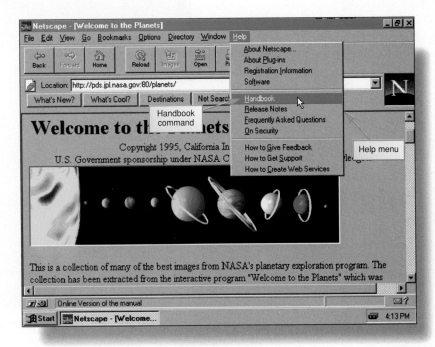

FIGURE 1-64

> **More** *About* **Printing Selected Pages**
>
> Clicking Print Preview on the File menu will display the formatted Web page as it will print on the printer. This allows you to see each page and select the appropriate page number to use when printing only selected pages.

2 **Click Handbook. Using the scroll box on the scroll bar, scroll down the page.**

The Netscape Navigator Handbook page displays (Figure 1-65). The Handbook contains hypertext links to useful, informative documents such as menu item descriptions and other reference materials. An alphabetical Index displays near the bottom of the page. Information about saving will be found under the letter S.

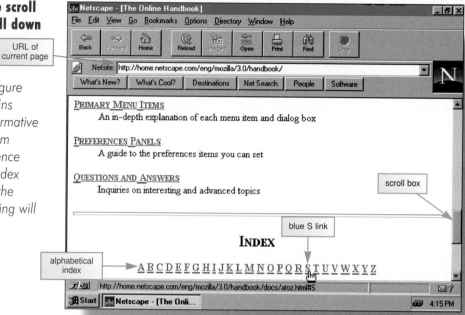

FIGURE 1-65

3 **Click the blue S link.**

A page displays with Help links to topics beginning with the letter S (Figure 1-66). The How can I save files and images onto my hard disk? topic contains information on saving.

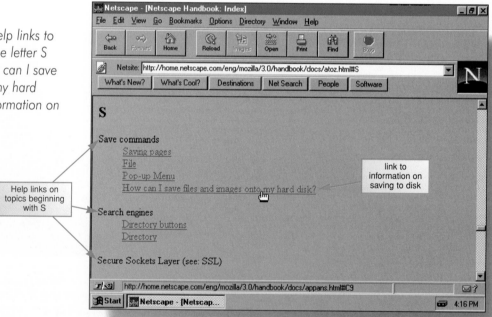

FIGURE 1-66

4 **Click the How can I save files and images onto my hard disk? link.**

Information on saving displays (Figure 1-67). You can return to the Index using the Back button on the toolbar and search the alphabetical index for other topics of interest. Use the scroll box to display more information about saving information to disk.

saving to disk information displays

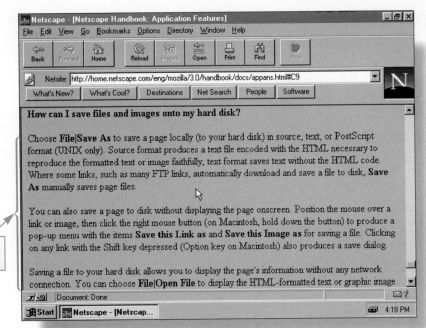

FIGURE 1-67

The previous steps used the Handbook command on the Help menu to obtain Help. Table 1-1 summarizes the commands on the Help menu shown in Figure 1-64 on page NN 1.43.

OtherWays

1. Press ALT+H, press letter H

TABLE 1-1

MENU COMMAND	FUNCTION
About Netscape	Displays information about the Netscape program.
About Plug-ins	Displays information about special application programs that can be used along with Netscape.
Registration Information	Displays information about registering Netscape.
Software	Displays information about new releases of Netscape.
Handbook	Displays menus of Help topics.
Release Notes	Displays information about the current release of Netscape.
Frequently Asked Questions	Displays answers to frequently asked questions.
On Security	Displays information about sending secured information over the Internet.
How to Give Feedback	Describes how to send mail to the Netscape Communications Corporation.
How to Get Support	Describes how to obtain technical support.
How to Create Web Services	Describes how to create your own Web site.

More *About* **the Handbook**

The Handbook Web page contains links to useful topics such as an Internet tutorial, HTML formatting language, and Internet security.

Exiting Netscape

After you have browsed the World Wide Web and learned how to manage Web pages, you can exit Netscape and return control to Windows 95. Perform the steps on the next page to exit Netscape.

Steps To Exit Netscape

1 Point to the Close button in the title bar (Figure 1-68).

2 Click to return to the Windows 95 desktop.

The Windows 95 desktop redisplays.

> **OtherWays**
> 1. On File menu click Exit
> 2. Press ALT+F, press letter X
> 3. Double-click Control-menu icon in title bar

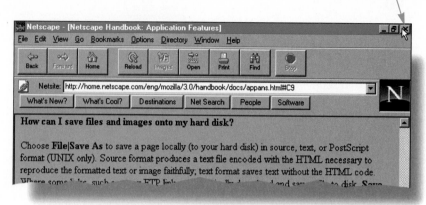

FIGURE 1-68

Project Summary

After completing Project 1, you now have enough knowledge of Netscape basics to answer confidently the questions of patrons of the Milschester Library. In this project, you learned about the Internet, the World Wide Web, hypertext documents, and URLs. You learned how to follow hypertext links and display Web pages. You then learned how to use Netscape's history list and how to create and use bookmarks. Using the techniques just presented, saving and printing images and Web pages were discussed. Finally, you learned how to use Netscape's online Help.

What You Should Know

Having completed this project, you now should be able to perform the following tasks:

▶ Access Help in Netscape *(NN 1.43)*
▶ Add a Bookmark to the Bookmark List *(NN 1.24)*
▶ Browse the World Wide Web by Entering a URL *(NN 1.15)*
▶ Copy and Paste a Section of a Web Page into Notepad *(NN 1.37)*
▶ Display a Web Page Using the History List *(NN 1.23)*
▶ Exit Netscape *(NN 1.46)*
▶ Import a Bookmark List from a Floppy Disk *(NN 1.31)*
▶ Move Back and Forth in the History List *(NN 1.21)*
▶ Print a Web Page *(NN 1.41)*

▶ Reload a Page *(NN 1.20)*
▶ Remove a Bookmark from the Bookmark List *(NN 1.29)*
▶ Retrieve a Web Page Using a Bookmark *(NN 1.26)*
▶ Save a Bookmark List to a Floppy Disk *(NN 1.27)*
▶ Save the Notepad Document and Exit Notepad *(NN 1.40)*
▶ Save a Picture on a Web Page *(NN 1.34)*
▶ Save a Web Page *(NN 1.33)*
▶ Start Netscape *(NN 1.11)*
▶ Start Notepad *(NN 1.36)*
▶ Stop a Page in Transfer *(NN 1.19)*

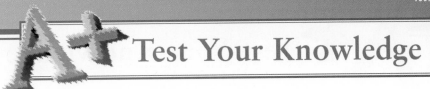

Test Your Knowledge

1 True/False

Instructions: Circle T if the statement is true or F if the statement is false.

T   F   1. One or more connected computer systems, terminals, and communications technologies is called a link.

T   F   2. Hypermedia is accessed by clicking certain words or pictures designated as links.

T   F   3. Browsers relieve you from having to remember the syntax of complex commands needed to connect to computers on the Internet.

T   F   4. The title of the current page in the Netscape display area is shown in the location text box.

T   F   5. A typical URL (Uniform Resource Locator) is composed of two parts, a title and hypermedia address.

T   F   6. The domain name is the Internet address of a computer on the Internet.

T   F   7. To select a hypertext link to follow, you simply click the link.

T   F   8. The history list provides a permanent record of the Web pages you visit.

T   F   9. The Back and Forward buttons are used to traverse through the bookmark list.

T   F   10. You can save the text portion of Web pages, but not the pictures.

2 Multiple Choice

Instructions: Circle the correct answer.

1. The collection of hypertext links throughout the Internet create an interconnected network of links called the _____.
   a. World Hypermedia Network
   b. Information Superhighway
   c. World Wide Web
   d. World InternetWork

2. The starting point for most Web sites is called a(n) _____.
   a. browser
   b. URL
   c. root directory
   d. home page

3. An item that is not part of the Netscape window is a(n) _____.
   a. menu bar
   b. format button
   c. toolbar
   d. status indicator

(continued)

Test Your Knowledge

Multiple Choice *(continued)*

4. The address of Web pages at Web sites on the World Wide Web is called a(n) _____.
   a. Uniform Resource Locator
   b. Internet address
   c. domain name
   d. folder

5. You can identify a hypertext link because the _____.
   a. link is in reverse video
   b. computer beeps when the mouse pointer is moved over the link
   c. color of the link changes when the mouse pointer is moved over it
   d. mouse pointer changes to a pointing hand when moved over the link

6. If you want a fresh copy of the Web page in the display area, click the _____.
   a. Stop button with a red icon on the toolbar
   b. Reload button on the toolbar
   c. Back button on the toolbar
   d. status indicator containing the Netscape corporate logo

7. The Netscape menu that allows you to retrieve permanently stored URLs is called _____.
   a. Bookmarks
   b. Go
   c. View
   d. File

8. To print a Web page, use either Print on the File menu or click the _____ button on the toolbar.
   a. Find
   b. What's Cool
   c. Print
   d. Reload

9. To save a picture from a Web page, right-click the _____.
   a. Images button
   b. Help menu
   c. location text box
   d. picture

10. Documents containing topics such as Internet basics, a Netscape tutorial, and an alphabetical index can be found by _____.
    a. clicking File on the menu bar
    b. clicking the Back button on the toolbar
    c. clicking Help on the menu bar
    d. clicking the status indicator containing the Netscape corporate logo

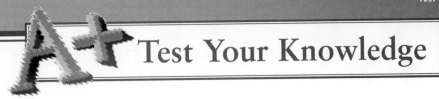

A+ Test Your Knowledge

3 Understanding the Netscape Window

Instructions: In Figure 1-69, arrows point to the major components of the Netscape window. Identify the various parts of the window in the spaces provided.

FIGURE 1-69

4 Understanding Toolbar Buttons

Instructions: In Figures 1-70 and 1-71 on the next page, arrows point to several buttons on the Netscape toolbar. In the spaces provided, briefly explain the purpose of each button.

FIGURE 1-70

(continued)

 Test Your Knowledge

Understanding Toolbar Buttons (*continued*)

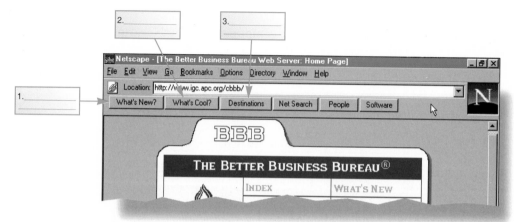

FIGURE 1-71

5 Understanding Bookmarks

Instructions: Using the Netscape window in Figure 1-72, list the steps to create a bookmark for the Mortal Kombat page.

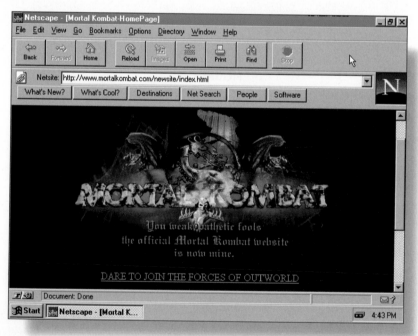

FIGURE 1-72

1. _____
2. _____
3. _____

Use Help

1 Using Netscape Help

Instructions: Start Netscape and perform the following tasks with a computer:

1. Click the Handbook directory button.
2. Scroll down to the alphabetical index at the bottom of the page.
3. Using the index, find and display information about the View menu, as shown in Figure 1-73.
4. Write a brief explanation of each command that appears on the View menu, including an example of when you would use the command. Turn in the explanations to your instructor.

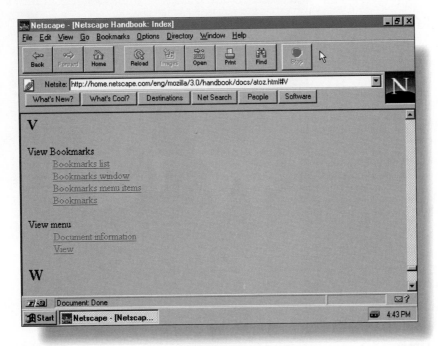

FIGURE 1-73

2 Using Netscape Help to Find Information

Instructions: Start Netscape and perform the following tasks with a computer:

1. Using the Netscape Help menu, answer the following questions:
   a. What is the release level of the Netscape program you are using? _____
   b. What are some of the new features of Netscape? _____
   c. How are SLIP and PPP connections used on the Internet? _____
   d. What is JAVA? _____

In the Lab

1 Printing a Graphical Image

Instructions: Start Netscape and perform the following tasks with a computer:

1. Type `http://www.atmos.uiuc.edu` into the location text box. This will contact the University of Illinois weather center.
2. Click the Weather Visualizer link.
3. Click the Satellite Imagery link.
4. Fill in the form to display a color-enhanced infrared image of the weather in your area as shown in Figure 1-74.
5. Print the weather map, write your name on the picture and turn it in to your instructor.

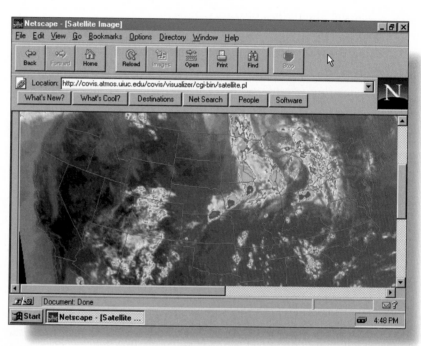

FIGURE 1-74

2 Saving a Web Page on a Floppy Disk

Instructions: Start Netscape and perform the following tasks with a computer:

1. Replace the URL in the location text box with http://www.purdue.edu/DFA and then retrieve the page shown in Figure 1-75. This will contact Purdue University's Financial Aid Web site.
2. Scroll down the page to find what three general types of financial aid are available.

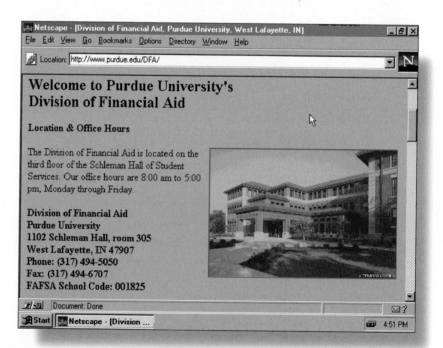

FIGURE 1-75

In the Lab

3. Save the Web page containing the financial aid information on a floppy disk in drive A or B.
4. Print only the first page of the Web page, write your name on the page and turn it in to your instructor.

3 Managing Bookmarks

Instructions: Start Netscape and perform the following tasks with a computer:

1. Click the What's Cool button to retrieve the What's Cool Web page, as shown in Figure 1-76.
2. Scroll down the Web page and browse through some of the links on the page.
3. When you find a Web page that interests you, add the URL to the bookmark list.
4. Retrieve the Web page again using the bookmark.
5. Remove the bookmark.
6. Verify that the bookmark is deleted.
7. Print the first page of the interesting Web page, write your name on it along with the steps to create and remove a bookmark, and turn it in to your instructor.

FIGURE 1-76

4 Cutting and Pasting Using the Clipboard

Instructions: Start Netscape and perform the following tasks with a computer:

1. Replace the URL in the location text box with http://www.careermosaic.com and retrieve the page shown in Figure 1-77 on the next page.
2. Click the Career Resource Center link.
3. Scroll down and follow the links to display tips on cover letters.

(continued)

In the Lab

Cutting and Pasting Using the Clipboard *(continued)*

4. Copy a sample cover letter to the Clipboard and then insert the Clipboard contents into Windows Notepad. *Hint:* Press and hold down the SHIFT key while dragging over the text. This allows you to scroll down without loosing the previously high-lighted text. Release the SHIFT button when the entire letter is highlighted.

5. Type your name in the sample cover letter.

6. Save the Notepad file to a floppy disk in drive A or B.

7. Print the Notepad file and turn it in to your instructor.

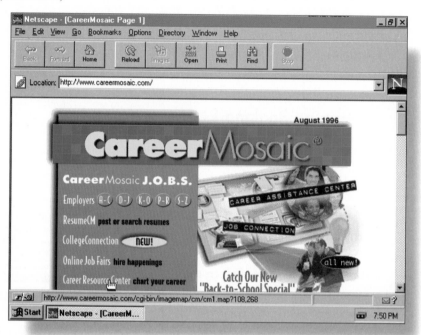

FIGURE 1-77

5 Saving a Graphical Image on a Floppy Disk

Instructions: Start Netscape and perform the following tasks with a computer:

1. Replace the URL in the location text box with http://www.studio.sgi.com/Gallery/ and display the page shown in Figure 1-78. This will contact Silicon Graphics Corporation.

2. Scroll down the page until the five rooms image displays. Click one of the rooms.

3. Follow the links until you display a picture that interests you.

4. Save the picture on a floppy disk in drive A or B.

5. Print the image, write your name on it and turn it in to your instructor.

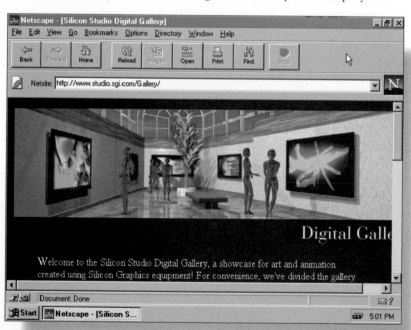

FIGURE 1-78

In the Lab

6 Connecting to the Shelly Cashman Online Home Page

Instructions: Start Netscape and perform the following tasks with a computer. Additional exercises for this project are available at the Shelly Cashman Online World Wide Web site. Perform the following steps to access these exercises. With Netscape on the screen, click the location text box. Type http://www.scseries.com in the location text box and then press ENTER. Scroll down and click Student Center. Scroll down and click Netscape Navigator 3 Running Under Windows 95. Scroll down and click Project 1 Introduction to Netscape. Complete the activities listed.

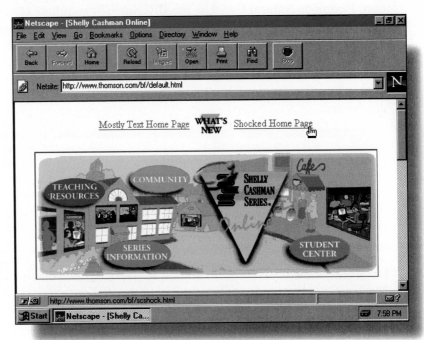

FIGURE 1-79

Cases and Places

The difficulty of these case studies varies:

▶ Case studies preceded by a single half moon are the least difficult. You are asked to perform the exercise based on techniques learned in the project.
▶▶ Case studies preceded by two half moons are more difficult. You must perform the exercise and carry out calculations.
▶▶▶ Case studies preceded by three half moons are the most difficult. You must perform the exercise by obtaining and organizing the necessary information and then prepare a report.

1 ▶ You are doing research on the computer industry, and want to see if there are any late-breaking stories. Using Netscape, connect to http://www.pcweek.com to connect to PC Week on-line magazine. Find an interesting computer news story. Print the story and turn it in to your instructor.

Cases and Places

2 ▶ An uncle of yours is thinking about investing in the stock market. He has asked you to find the ticker names and prices for the following stocks: Bethlehem Steel; Netscape Communications Corporation; Piedmont Natural Gas. Use the URL http://www.quote.com/ticker.html to connect to a Web site that displays ticker symbols based on company names to obtain the ticker symbol for the three stocks. Type in the name of the company in the text box and click the Search button. After obtaining the ticker symbol, use the following URL http://quotes.galt.com/cgi-bin/stockclnt to display a Web page with a text box in which you type the ticker symbol to display the current price of each stock. Note whether the stock pays a dividend, and the amount of the dividend. Turn in the list of stock prices and dividends.

3 ▶ The old truck you were driving broke down and you are in the market for a new one. Prices for new trucks depend on the size of the truck and any options. Use the URL http://www.dealernet.com/winacar.html to connect to Dealernet and then click New Cars to search for a new truck. Check the local availability and prices for compact trucks, large trucks, and utility vehicles from several manufacturers. Print a page containing some of the results and turn it in.

4 ▶▶ Your family is planning a vacation to Mexico. Everyone in the family wants to go to a different Mexican city, but funds are limited. Using the URL http://mexicana.ms.wwa.com/english/traveller connect to the Web site and click the Trip Calculator link. Use the Trip Calculator to calculate the cost to stay seven nights for four different Mexican cities. Choose the origin city closest to where you live. Try several different hotels and several different dates to get the best price. Turn in a list of the dates, cities, and prices.

5 ▶▶▶ Netscape is the most popular Web browser program, utilized by almost 80% of Web users. Netscape, however, was not the first Web browser. This claim is held by Mosaic, from the National Center for Super-Computing Applications. Today, browsers can be purchased, included with Internet provider software, or obtained free from the Internet. Find out about three other Web browser programs. Write a brief report describing the features of each browser, pointing out their similarities and differences.

6 ▶▶▶ Before the Web, the Internet was accessed through the use of several service programs. Each service program provided one type of activity, or service, using a unique vocabulary of commands. This made using the Internet difficult for the casual user. You had to know which service program, and which particular command to use. Find out about four of the traditional Internet service programs and write a report briefly describing each one, what the service program was used for, and a sample of some of the commands used with the service program.

7 ▶▶▶ When printed, some Web pages can span several pieces of paper. There will be times when you will want to print only the one page containing the information in which you are interested. Using the handbook, find out how to determine the page number of a multi-page Netscape printout and how to print only that page. Write the complete set of instructions for finding the page number of, and printing a particular page of a hypertext document, and turn it in to your instructor.

Netscape Navigator 3

Windows 95

Information Mining Using Web Search Engines

Objectives:

You will have mastered the material in this project when you can:

▶ Search the Web using the Internet Directory
▶ Search the Web using AltaVista
▶ Search the Web using Infoseek
▶ Set search and display options in Lycos
▶ Search the Web using Lycos
▶ Search the Web using WebCrawler
▶ Retrieve files using FTP
▶ Retrieve files using gopher

Project 2

Searching for GOLD on the Tangled WEB

Or, Where in the World...?

Say you just have been admitted to the largest and, arguably, the most diverse and complete library in the universe. Millions of pages of information are at your disposal, with no overdue fees to pay. Eager to begin your quest for knowledge, you scan your surroundings, vainly searching for the card catalog that will lead you to your first topic of interest. But none is to be found. With mounting trepidation, you look for librarians, a help desk, or clerks. Your search is futile. A quick perusal of the shelves confirms your fear: the items are in no particular order. Nothing is arranged alphabetically, chronologically, or in any fashion you can fathom. How can you escape this nightmare?

This scenario is similar to what you encounter looking through the estimated 22 million pages (and growing) of information on the World Wide Web. Fortunately, the computer industry is innovative and quick to respond to its adherents' urgent needs. To assist users in their searches of the Web, nifty devices known as search engines

were developed. They bring order to the chaos of the Web by indexing the vast amount of information.

Search engines are to the World Wide Web what a card catalog is to a library. They allow the user quickly to search and locate specific topics on the Web, much as a library card catalog guides patrons to the correct location of printed information. Most search engines share a common method of locating information: the *keyword*. A user types a word or phrase, such as aviation or global warming, and the search engine scans the sites on the Web to find matches, or *hits*.

While many search engines exist and are readily available to Web users, several are well known and widely used. One of the more popular is the Yahoo Directory, which you will use in this project. Yahoo is praised as being the fastest and most current because it is updated daily.

Another favorite search engine is AltaVista, developed by Digital Equipment Corporation. Containing what Digital claims is the largest Web index, AltaVista can perform detailed searches for any type of information sought. Because it is so large, however, searching for hits can be time consuming. Other touted search engines are Excite, C/net, Magellan, Lycos, Infoseek, and WebCrawler.

One search engine differs in its approach to finding information on the Web. Excite uses concept-based navigation on the Web. This unique approach, though slower and more likely to return irrelevant information, can perform more abstract searches. Rather than using Civil War as a keyword, for example, you could type, What caused the Civil War?

Currently, search engines are being heralded as the saviors of searching the tangled Web. They have spawned a multibillion dollar industry, and competition is fierce. On the horizon, faster and more accurate search engines are forthcoming.

Project 2

Netscape Navigator 3

Windows 95

Case Perspective

People who visit the library usually have some idea of what they are looking for. They do not always know exactly in what resource they will find it, however. Fortunately, libraries have card catalogs that simplify the search. Some word or words would be chosen that closely identifies the topic of interest. These words would be used to search through the card catalog. If nothing useful was found, some modification of the words is done, and another search, perhaps in some other area of the card catalog, is performed. This continues until the desired information is found.

Similar Web page catalogs exist on the World Wide Web that can be searched for information. Special programs called search engines are used to access these Web page catalogs. Your job, as the computer specialist for the Milschester Library, is to become as proficient in using Web search engines to search the World Wide Web as the other librarians are in searching the library's card catalog.

Information Mining Using Web Search Engines

Introduction

The World Wide Web is growing rapidly every day. The problems of finding the information you seek, usually associated with using the original Internet service programs, are starting to surface with the Web as well.

In Project 2, you will learn how to use searching tools created specifically for use on the World Wide Web. In addition, access to traditional non-Web searching and file transfer tools will be shown.

Web Search Engines

One of the difficult problems with the Internet before the creation of the World Wide Web was finding the files and information in which you were interested. Some primitive Internet search tools such as archie, gopher, and WAIS were developed to address the problem, but even with these tools, you had to learn a command language to use them. Still, using these tools was better than connecting to computer after computer on the Internet and searching through disk directory after disk directory.

Several **search tools** have been developed for searching the World Wide Web. These tools, also called **search engines**, allow you to search the Web in terms of what you want, instead of where it is located. Most of the search tools are made available as Web pages with an input form in which you type **keywords** (a word or phrase) representing topics of items to search for.

Why study several different search tools? Just as it is impossible for a card catalog to contain an entry for every book in the world, it is impossible for each search engine to catalog every Web page on the World Wide Web. In addition, different search tools on the Web perform different types of searches. Some require keywords in the title of Web pages. Others scan hypertext links for the keywords. Still others search the entire text of Web pages. Because of the different searching techniques, the results of the search can sometimes be surprising.

The developers of Netscape realized the need for a searching mechanism and created a Web page containing access to several of the more popular tools. The following sections show how to start Netscape and access Web searching tools.

Starting Netscape

Start Netscape following the procedure you used at the beginning of Project 1 on page NN 1.10. This step is summarized below.

TO START NETSCAPE

Step 1: With the Windows 95 desktop active, double-click the Netscape shortcut icon.

The Netscape window with the Netscape home page displays (Figure 2-1). The Netscape home page might display differently on your computer because of continuous changes and updates.

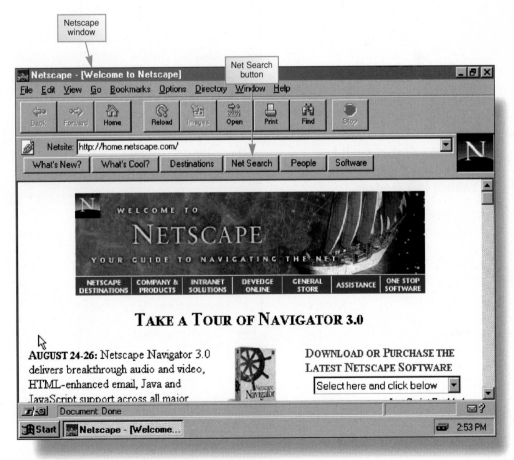

FIGURE 2-1

Accessing the Web Search Tools Page

Because searching is a frequently used method of finding information on the Web, Netscape made accessing the Web search tools page easy, as shown in the following steps.

Steps To Access Web Search Tools

1 **Click the Net Search button.**

The Net Search Web page displays (Figure 2-2). The URL of the Net Search Web page displays in the location text box. A URL is the address of a Web page. Further down the page, the Net Search page contains links to several Web search tools.

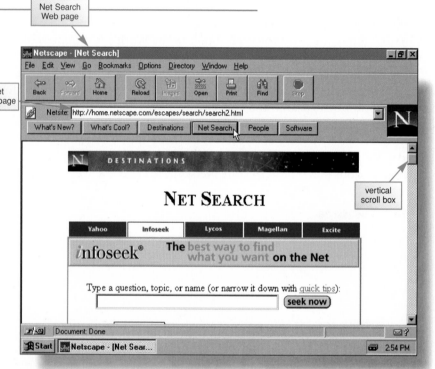

FIGURE 2-2

2 **Using the vertical scroll bar, scroll down the page until the YAHOO! link displays.**

The YAHOO! link displays (Figure 2-3).

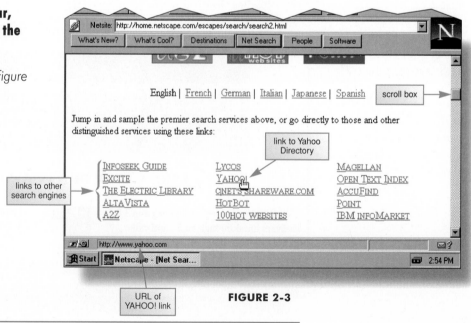

FIGURE 2-3

OtherWays

1. On Directory menu click Internet Search

In Figure 2-3, you can see that several search engines are available. This project explores five of these search engines to show you how you can perform an electronic search for information on the Web. The first of the search engines, called the Yahoo Directory, uses a series of menus to organize information.

Searching the Web Using the Yahoo Directory

The **Yahoo Directory** uses a series of menus to organize links to Web pages without requiring that you enter any search keywords. Starting with general categories and becoming increasingly more specific as links are selected, the Yahoo Directory provides a menu-like interface for searching the Web.

To illustrate using the Yahoo Directory, assume you are writing a paper about dyslexia for your nursing class and want to find some information about the condition. To begin the search, display the Yahoo Directory Web page as shown in the following steps.

Steps To Display the Yahoo Directory Web Page

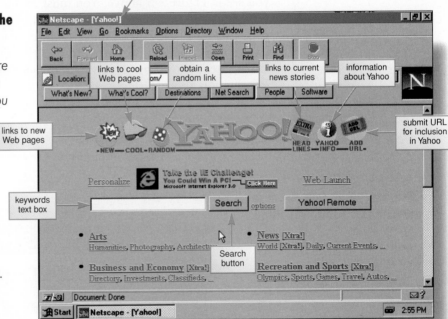

1 **Click the blue YAHOO! link on the Net Search page.**

The YAHOO! page displays (Figure 2-4). The small pictures at the top of the page are links that allow you to perform activities such as submit a URL for addition to the Yahoo Directory, request a random link, and obtain Help. The text box is used for entering keywords, and a Search button initiates a search. Searching using keywords will be illustrated later in the project. The actual directory is further down the page.

FIGURE 2-4

2 **Scroll down the page to reveal the top-level Yahoo Directory list.**

The top-level Yahoo Directory displays (Figure 2-5). The directory is organized into broad categories. Each category is a link to a Web page containing more detailed topics about the broad category. Links to some of those detailed topics appear below the broad categories.

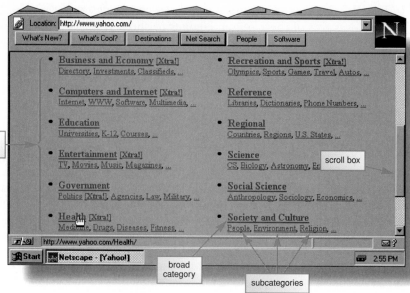

FIGURE 2-5

Web pages in the Yahoo Directory are organized into the broad categories you see in Figure 2-5 above. You must decide into which category your search topic falls and then click the corresponding link. When you click the link, another page of links displays with more specific topics from which to choose. You continue following the links until you find the information you are seeking. The following steps show how to navigate through the Yahoo Directory to retrieve information about dyslexia.

Steps **To Perform a Web Search Using the Yahoo Directory**

1 **Click the Health link, because dyslexia is a health condition.**

The Yahoo! - Health Web page displays (Figure 2-6).

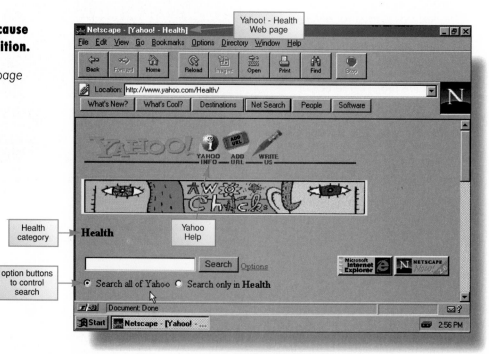

FIGURE 2-6

2 **Scroll down to reveal the list of Health links.**

The list of Health links displays (Figure 2-7). Notice the links represent different areas of health. The number next to the link indicates how many Web pages you will find if you click that link. The highlighted word NEW! to the right of a link indicates the link has been updated recently with new Web pages. The @ symbol at the end of some of the links indicates a link to a different Yahoo category. The Disabilities link is where information about dyslexia is likely to be found.

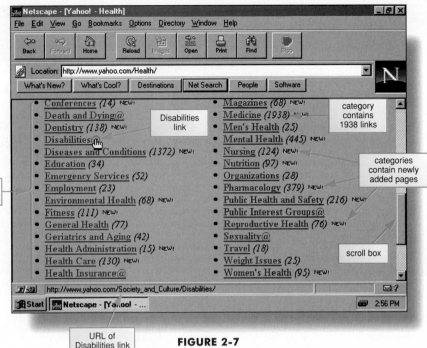

FIGURE 2-7

3 **Click the Disabilities link and then scroll down to reveal links to information about disabilities.**

The Yahoo! - Society and Culture:Disabilities Web page displays (Figure 2-8). The title indicates you have left the Health topic and moved to the Society and Culture topic. The links on this page represent different areas concerning disabilities. Notice the Dyslexia link. Twelve links are available on the Dyslexia page.

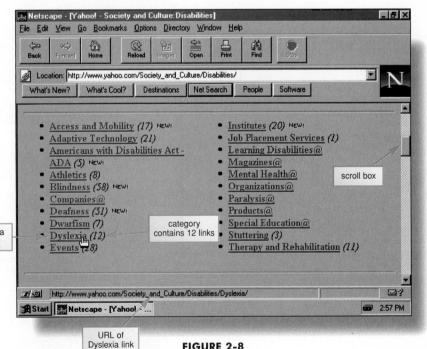

FIGURE 2-8

4 **Click the Dyslexia link and then scroll down to reveal the list of dyslexia links.**

The Yahoo! - Society and Culture:Disabilities:Dyslexia Web page displays (Figure 2-9). Notice the absence of numbers next to the links. This indicates the lowest level of the hierarchy of Yahoo menus. A brief explanation of the page appears next to each link.

positive
aspects link →

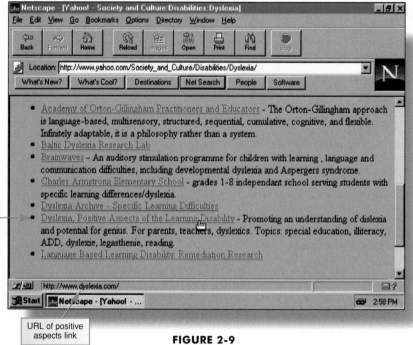

URL of positive
aspects link

FIGURE 2-9

title of
Web page

5 **Click the Dyslexia, Positive Aspects of the Learning Disability link.**

URL of
Web page

The Dyslexia, The Gift Web page displays (Figure 2-10). Scrolling down the page, you will find numerous links to information about dyslexia.

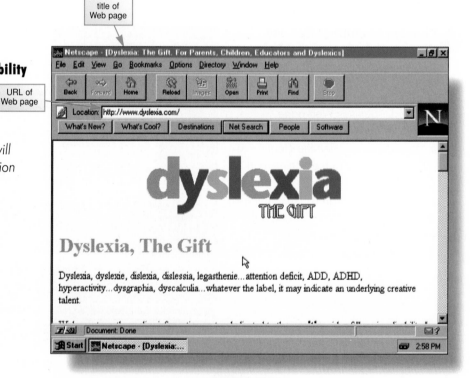

FIGURE 2-10

6 **Scroll down the page until the link What is the Positive Side of Dyslexia? displays. Point to the link.**

The URL of the Web page displays in the active link indicator (Figure 2-11).

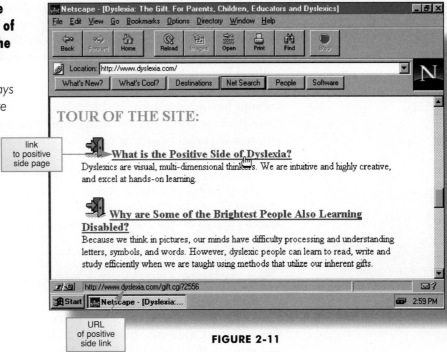

FIGURE 2-11

7 **Click the What is the Positive Side of Dyslexia? link.**

The What is the positive side of dyslexia? Web page displays (Figure 2-12). The page contains some of the good traits of dyslexic individuals.

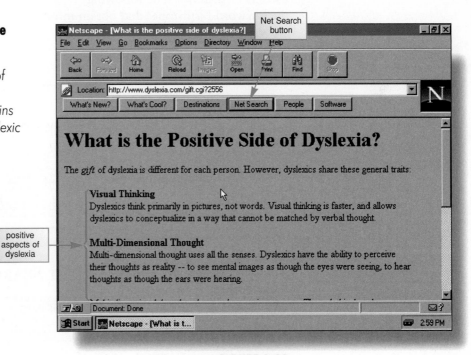

FIGURE 2-12

The Web page containing the positive traits now can be printed or saved on a floppy disk and used in your nursing class as a source for your paper. See the sections in Project 1 on page NN 1.41 for printing and page NN 1.33 for saving.

You have searched the World Wide Web using the menu-driven Yahoo directory. With the ability to pick from a list of topics, you do not have to provide any keywords to find information. You might have to spend considerable time traveling through several levels of menus, however, only to discover that nothing is available concerning your topic.

Other Web search engines will search the Web and display links to Web pages without having to maneuver through any intermediate pages. You provide one or more relevant keywords about the topic you are interested in, and the search engine will return links that point directly to Web pages that contain those keywords.

The search engines on the Netscape Net Search Web page use different searching techniques and search several types of Web resources. Because of this, it is wise to learn how to use more than one Web search engine. The first of the search engines on the Net Search Web page that uses keywords is Infoseek.

Searching the Web Using Infoseek

Infoseek is a Web search program made available from Infoseek Corporation in Santa Clara, California. Infoseek searches a database of computerized periodicals and more than 19,000,000 Web pages.

To illustrate using Infoseek, assume you are interested in the type of gems used as birthstones. The following steps show how to use Infoseek to search for the keyword birthstones and obtain information about the gems.

Steps To Perform a Web Search Using Infoseek

1 **Click the Net Search button to redisplay the Net Search Web page.**

The Net Search Web page displays (Figure 2-13). The Infoseek search form displays at the top of the page. The form contains a text box where you type the keywords for which to search, and a seek now button to start the search. If necessary, click the Infoseek button to display the Infoseek search form.

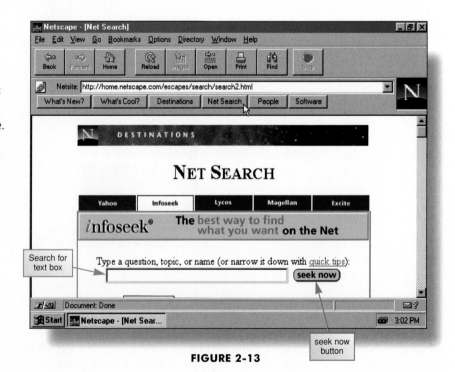

FIGURE 2-13

More About Infoseek

If you find a search result that you're interested in, you can search for similar pages by clicking Similar Pages. Infoseek Guide uses information about the selected page to search for other pages with similar content.

2 **Click the text box to display an insertion point. Type** birthstones **in the text box.**

The keyword birthstones displays in the text box (Figure 2-14). Notice the Yahoo-like directory of links.

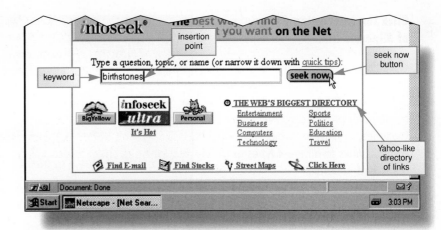

FIGURE 2-14

3 **Click the seek now button.**

*After a brief period of time, the Infoseek Guide: birthstones Web page displays (Figure 2-15). The page contains the word or phrase used in the search. Next, the total number of successful matches, or **hits**, and the number of hits displayed on the page are listed.*

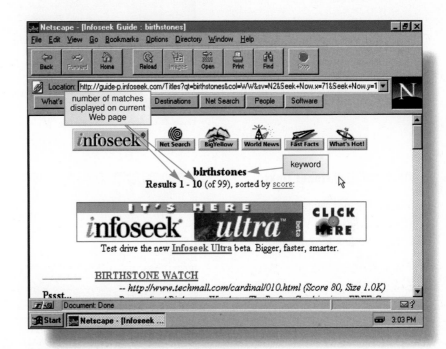

FIGURE 2-15

4 **Scroll down the page until the Interesting Groupings of Minerals link displays.**

Information about Web pages containing the word, birthstones, displays (Figure 2-16). Each hit consists of a link to the Web page, the URL of the Web page, a search score used to order the hits, the size of the Web page, and the first few lines of text from the Web page.

FIGURE 2-16

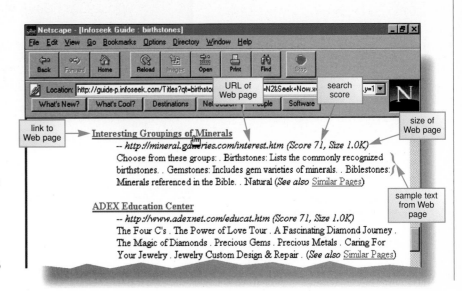

5 Click the Interesting Groupings of Minerals link.

The Interesting Groupings of Minerals Web page displays (Figure 2-17). This Web page is located on a computer provided by Amethyst Galleries, in Dayton, Ohio. It contains links to different types of gems and minerals.

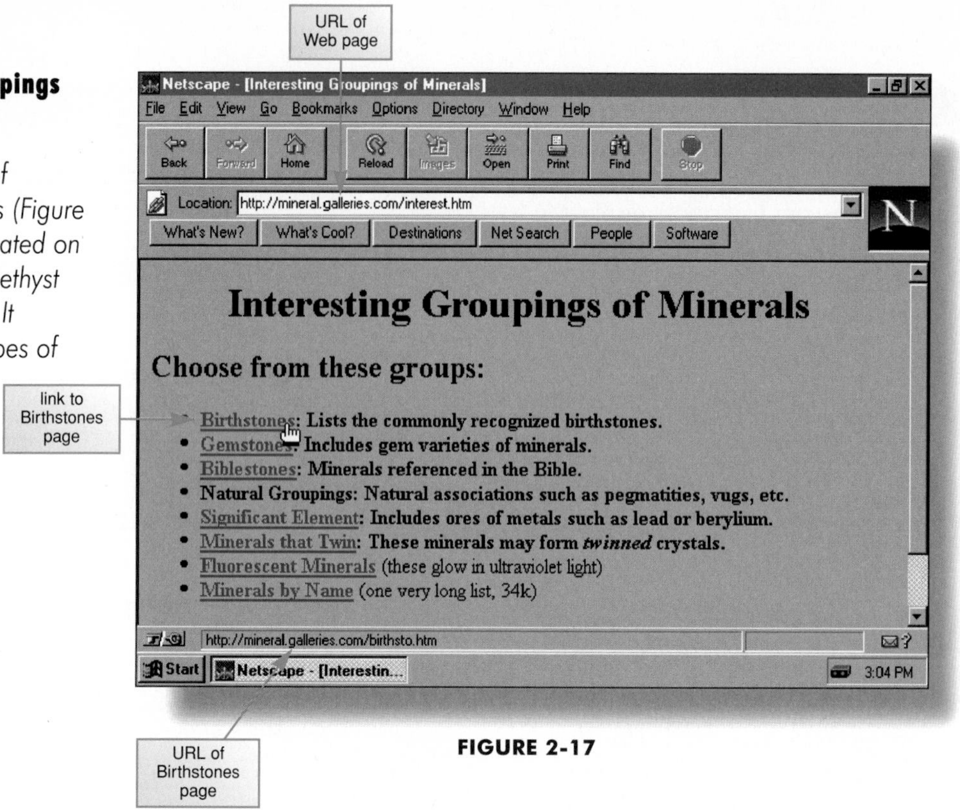

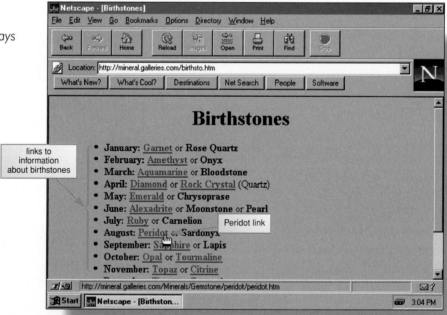

URL of
Web page

link to
Birthstones
page

URL of
Birthstones
page

FIGURE 2-17

6 Click the Birthstones links.

The Birthstones Web page displays (Figure 2-18). This Web page contains a link for each month of the year.

links to
information
about birthstones

FIGURE 2-18

7 **Click the Peridot link.**

Information about the mineral peridot displays (Figure 2-19). A larger picture of the mineral can be displayed by clicking the thumbnail picture.

thumbnail picture

information about peridot

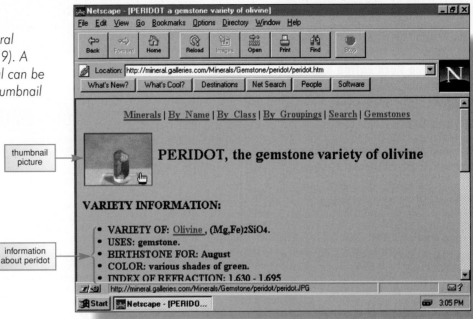

FIGURE 2-19

JPEG image

8 **Click the thumbnail picture.**

A large picture of a sample of peridot displays (Figure 2-20). This is a JPEG image (pronounced jay-peg). **JPEG,** *which stands for Joint Photographics Expert Group, is a method of encoding pictures on computers. The numbers 320x240 indicate the number of pixels, or picture elements, that make up the image. A* **pixel** *is the smallest addressable point on the CRT screen.*

Back button

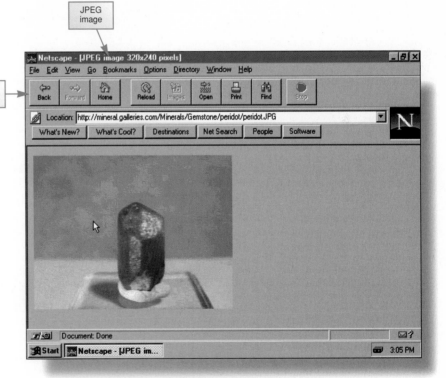

FIGURE 2-20

Remember in Figure 2-15 on page NN 2.13 only 10 titles out of 99 were displayed. If you did not find useful information in the first 10 links, you can request that the next set of 10 links out of the 99 be displayed, as shown in the steps on the next page.

Steps To Display the Next Set of Infoseek Search Results

1 Click the Back button until the Infoseek Guide: birthstones Web page redisplays.

The Infoseek Guide : birthstones Web page redisplays (Figure 2-21).

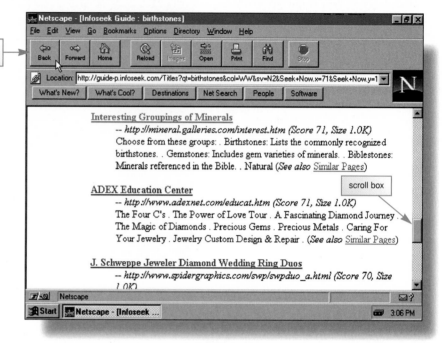

FIGURE 2-21

2 Scroll down the page until the link to the next 10 results displays.

The Next 10 Results (11 - 20) link displays (Figure 2-22). Most Web search engines present lists of matches this way, a few at a time, instead of listing them all at once. Some Web search engines allow you to control how many hits to display at one time.

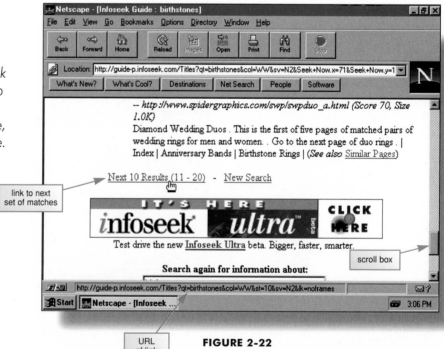

FIGURE 2-22

③ **Click the Next 10 Results (11 - 20) link.**

The Infoseek Guide birthstones Web page redisplays indicating it contains the next ten titles (Figure 2-23). The link to the previous 10 results allows you to go back and redisplay them, if necessary, by clicking the Previous 10 Results link. A new search can be performed by clicking the New Search link.

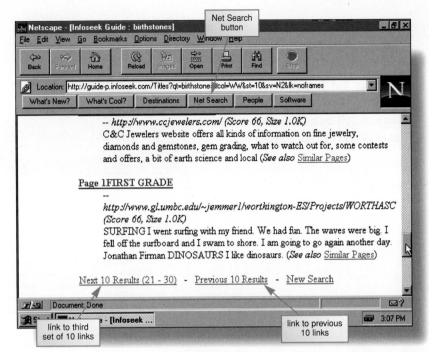

FIGURE 2-23

Other Ways

1. On Go menu click line containing Infoseek Net Search Results page

You can see how easy it is to find information about specific topics such as birthstones using Infoseek and following a few hypertext links. The page containing the information about peridot now can be saved on a floppy disk or printed. See the sections in Project 1 on page NN 1.33 for saving and page NN 1.41 for printing.

You can click another link if the first link did not provide the desired results, or click the New Search link to enter different keywords. You also can redisplay the Netscape Search page to use one of the other available search tools, such as AltaVista, which claims to have the largest searchable index of Web pages on the World Wide Web.

Searching the Web Using AltaVista

AltaVista is one of the newer search engines that provides searching capabilities for several different World Wide Web resources. AltaVista is made available from Digital Equipment Corporation.

To demonstrate the AltaVista search engine, assume you are giving an informational speech on stock derivatives and want to find out how these financial instruments work. The steps on the next page show how to use AltaVista to search for information about derivatives.

Steps To Display the AltaVista Web Page

1 **Click the Net Search button to redisplay the Net Search Web page. Scroll down the page until the ALTAVISTA link appears.**

The Net Search Web page displays (Figure 2-24).

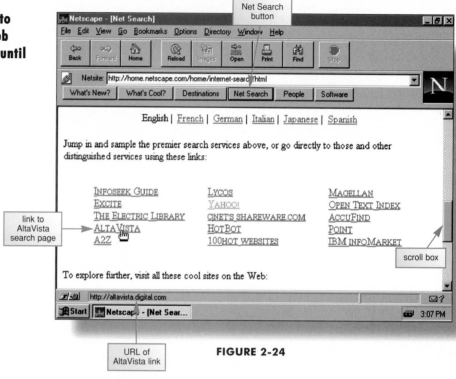

FIGURE 2-24

2 **Click the ALTAVISTA link.**

The AltaVista: Main Page Web page displays (Figure 2-25). The Web page contains images you can click to access resources such as help (Help), setting advanced search options (Advanced), or other AltaVista services. Under the images are two drop-down list boxes used to set search options, a text box where keywords are entered, and a Submit button to start the search.

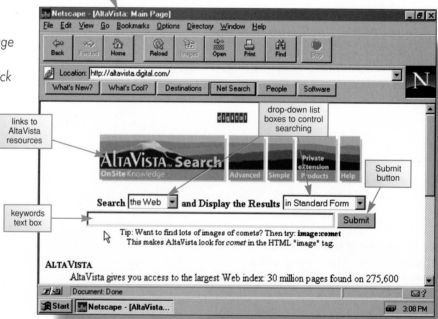

FIGURE 2-25

The AltaVista: Main Page Web page contains several small images at the top. Clicking the image labeled AltaVista displays the AltaVista home page. Clicking the Help image displays information about the AltaVista search engine. Clicking the Advanced image displays a form containing option buttons and drop-down list boxes that allow you to set options giving you greater control over your search. Clicking the Private eXtension Products image displays information about other AltaVista services.

The Search drop-down list box controls which Internet resources to look at when performing the search. The default resource is the Web, meaning that Web pages will be searched. The Display the Results drop-down list box controls how much detail is displayed for each successful match that is found. The default amount of detail is in Standard Form, which will be described later as a search is performed. The following steps show how to perform a Web search using AltaVista.

 Steps **To Search the Web Using AltaVista**

① Click the text box to display an insertion point. Type derivatives **in the text box.**

The keyword derivatives displays in the text box (Figure 2-26).

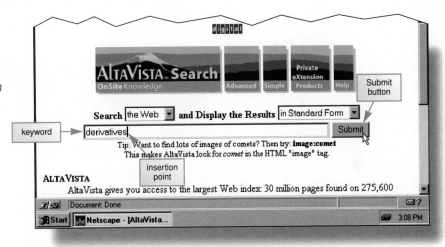

FIGURE 2-26

② Click the Submit button.

The AltaVista: Simple Query derivatives Web page displays (Figure 2-27). Notice AltaVista found more than 73,000 occurrences of the word derivatives in its index. About 40,000 Web pages in AltaVista's index contain the word, derivatives. The first set of 10 pages is listed.

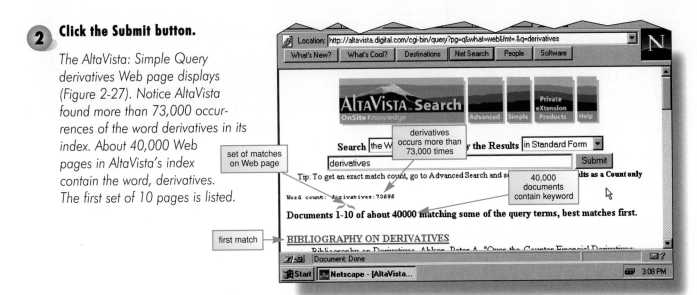

FIGURE 2-27

3 **Scroll down the page to reveal the results.**

Links to Web pages containing the keyword, derivatives, display (Figure 2-28). Some links to Web pages that contain the word, derivatives, display but none is related to financial vehicles. Figure 2-28 contains links to pine tar Web pages. You can see that sometimes the search results can be surprising. The keywords need to be more selective to eliminate these unrelated pages.

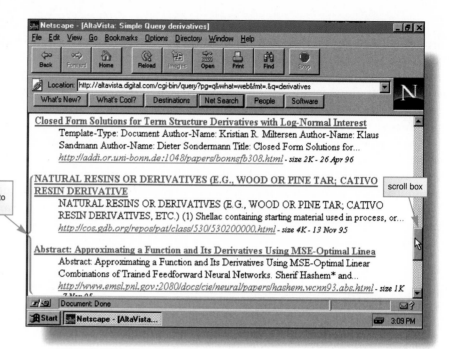

FIGURE 2-28

4 **Scroll back to the top of the page to reveal the keywords text box.**

The text box displays with the keyword, derivatives. Because the desired information is about financial derivatives, better results would be obtained by including the word financial in the keywords. In addition, some other keyword, such as definition, should be included to indicate you want explanatory information.

5 **Click the text box to display an insertion point. Type** definition financial **to the left of the derivatives keyword. Be sure to separate each word with a space.**

The new keywords display in the text box (Figure 2-29). Most Web search engines allow you to refine the keywords used in the search by retyping, adding to, or subtracting from, them.

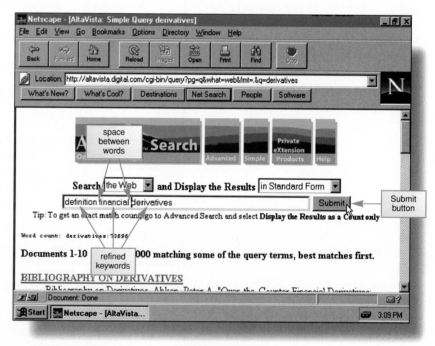

FIGURE 2-29

6 **Click the Submit button.**

The AltaVista: Simple Query definition financial derivatives Web page displays (Figure 2-30). Notice the number of times each term was found.

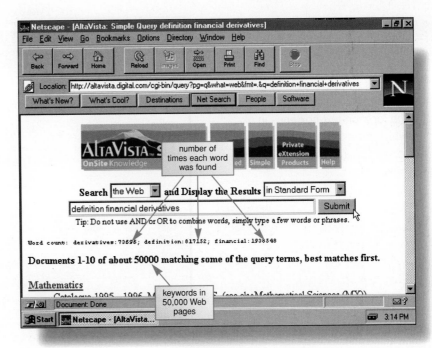

FIGURE 2-30

7 **Scroll down the page to reveal the results of the search.**

Links to Web pages containing the keywords, definition, financial derivatives, display (Figure 2-31). Each hit contains a link to the Web page, a summary of the contents of the page, the URL of the Web page, the size of the Web page, and the date it was added to the AltaVista index.

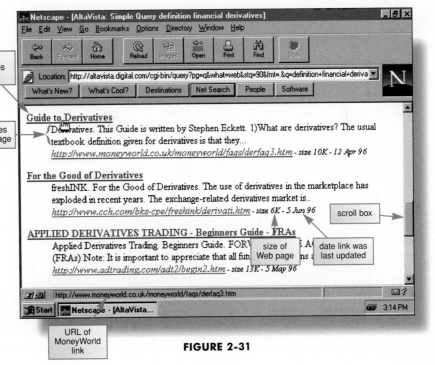

FIGURE 2-31

8 Click the Guide to Derivatives link.

The MoneyWorld Guides Web page displays (Figure 2-32). Notice the domain name portion of the URL in the location text box ends in uk, which means this Web page is located at a site in the United Kingdom.

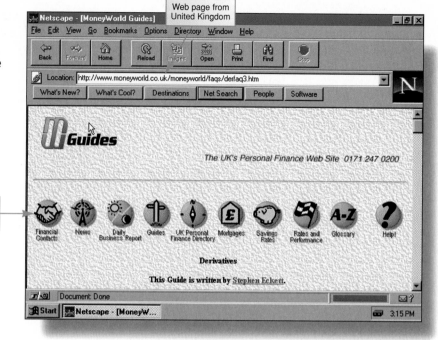

FIGURE 2-32

9 Scroll down to reveal more of the page.

*More information about financial derivatives displays (Figure 2-33). Documents in question-and-answer format often are referred to as **FAQs**, which is an acronym for frequently asked questions.*

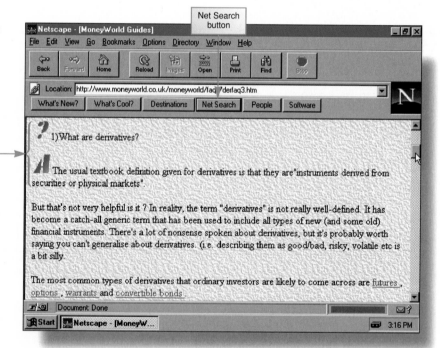

FIGURE 2-33

The derivatives page is organized in a question-and-answer format. You will find many documents like this on the World Wide Web. Referred to as **FAQs**, they are collections of **frequently asked questions** and associated answers about topics of interest. Most people trying to find certain information on the Internet are instructed to read the FAQs on that topic before asking for help. This prevents the same questions from being asked over and over again.

Most Web search engines allow you to refine the search by changing the keywords. You have successfully searched the Web using AltaVista. You can now return to the Netscape Net Search Web page to search the Web using another search tool.

Searching the Web Using Lycos

The next search engine, **Lycos**, searches not only the titles, but also the contents of Web pages for keywords. Lycos is provided and maintained by Lycos, Inc. from Wilmington, Maine. The Lycos search form contains several different options for controlling a Web search.

To illustrate using the Lycos search engine, assume you are doing an English research paper and need information about dangling modifiers. The following steps show how to use Lycos to find this information.

Displaying the Lycos Search Form

A link to the Lycos Search Form is available from the Netscape Net Search Web page. The following steps show how to display the Lycos Search Form.

 Steps To Display the Lycos Search Form

---

1 **Click the Net Search button to redisplay the Net Search Web page. Scroll down to reveal the LYCOS link.**

The Net Search Web page redisplays (Figure 2-34).

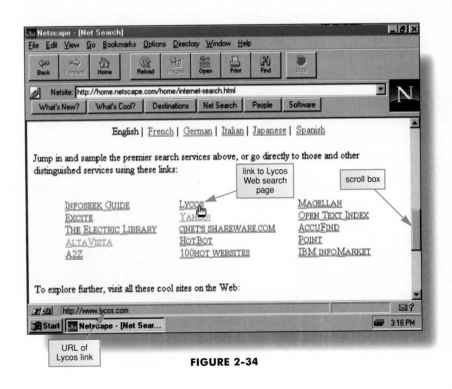

FIGURE 2-34

More *About* **Refining the Search**

You can force a search engine to search for a phrase of two or more words by placing the words within quotes. For example, using "financial derivatives" as keywords would only return hits if the two words were physically next to each other on the Web page.

2 **Click the LYCOS link.**

The Welcome to Lycos Web page displays (Figure 2-35). The Lycos page contains a text box for search keywords, a Go Get It button to initiate the search, and a link to advanced search options. Next on the page are several links to other Lycos services, such as current news, and adding a URL.

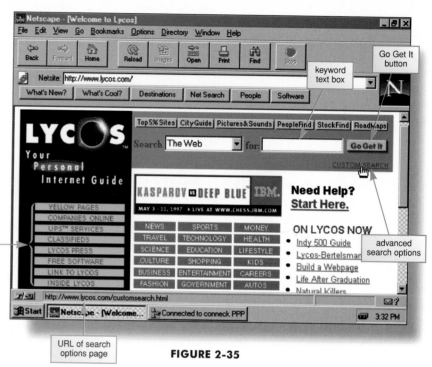

FIGURE 2-35

The Lycos search engine provides several options for customizing your search. You can control how the search is performed and how the results are displayed. The following step shows how to display the Lycos form containing advanced search options.

Steps **To Display the Lycos Search Options Form**

1 **Click the Customize your search link.**

The Lycos Search Form Web page displays (Figure 2-36). The search page contains a text box where keywords are entered, a Go Get It button to initiate the search, the Search Options drop-down list boxes that allow you to control how the search is performed, and the Display Options drop-down list boxes that control how the results are displayed. Clicking a box arrow displays a drop-down list box with available options.

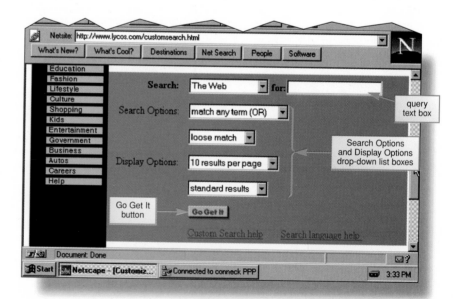

FIGURE 2-36

Figure 2-37 shows the Display Options available for displaying the results. The summary results option displays a small amount of detail about each matching Web page. The detailed results option displays a large amount of detail about each matching Web page. The standard results option is the default and is used in the examples in this project.

Figure 2-38 shows the Display Options available for controlling the number of successful matches, or hits, to display, with up to 40 matches returned at one time.

Figure 2-39 shows the Search Options available for controlling how keyword matches are made. The loose match option will return Web pages that match the keywords closely, but not exactly. This option returns more hits. The strong match option will return Web pages that match the keywords exactly. This option returns fewer hits. The loose match is the default and is used in the examples in this project.

Figure 2-40 shows the Search Options available for controlling how the keywords are handled during the matching process. The match all terms (AND) option means that all the keywords have to be found in the Web page for the match to be successful. The match all terms (OR) option means that only one or more of the keywords have to be found in the Web page for the match to be successful. The match 2 terms option means a successful match will occur if two out of three or more words in the keyword phrase are found in the Web page. For example, if the keywords, salmonella bacteria penicillin, were entered, any two of the three keywords appearing in a Web page would trigger a match. The last five options work similarly to the match 2 terms option.

Because you want to match both terms in the keywords, dangling modifiers, the Search Options should be changed from match all terms (OR) to match all terms (AND). The steps on the next page show how to change the options and perform the search.

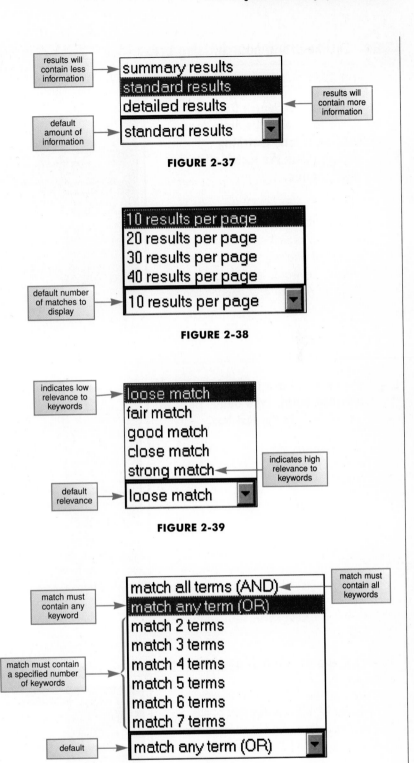

FIGURE 2-37

FIGURE 2-38

FIGURE 2-39

FIGURE 2-40

Steps To Perform a Search Using Lycos

1 **Click the first Search Options box arrow to display the drop-down list box of term matching options. Click the match all terms (AND) option.**

Match all terms (AND) becomes the default search option (Figure 2-41). Most Web search engines allow you to control whether the search for multiple keywords is performed using an AND or an OR condition.

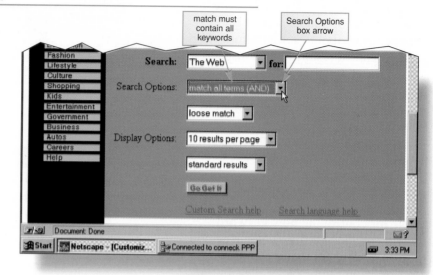

match must contain all keywords

Search Options box arrow

FIGURE 2-41

2 **Click the text box to display an insertion point. Type dangling modifiers in the text box.**

The keywords, dangling modifiers, display in the query text box (Figure 2-42).

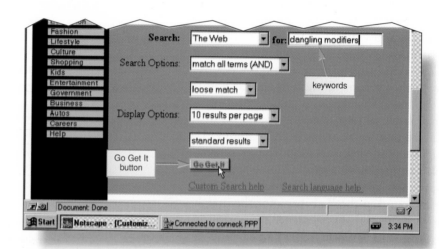

keywords

Go Get It button

FIGURE 2-42

3 **Click the Go Get It button.**

The results of the search display (Figure 2-43). The number of hits, or matches, to the keywords is 76. Only the first 10 are listed on the page.

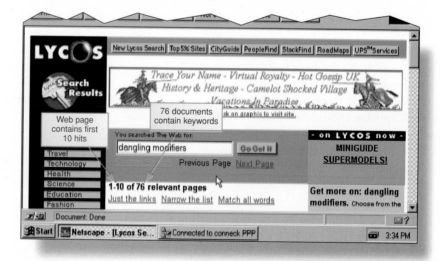

Web page contains first 10 hits

76 documents contain keywords

FIGURE 2-43

4 **Scroll down to reveal the links to the documents.**

The first matching document displays (Figure 2-44). The results consist of a number identifying this match, the link to the Web page, an outline and abstract of the contents of the Web page, the URL of the Web page, and the results of the match. This is the amount of information returned with standard results selected in the Display Options drop-down list box.

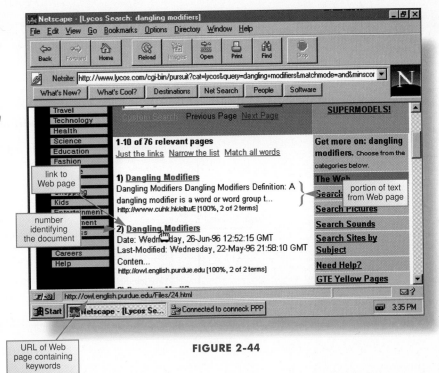

FIGURE 2-44

5 **Click the Dangling Modifiers link.**

The Dangling Modifiers Web page displays (Figure 2-45). The page is part of the writing assistance made available by the Writing Lab at Purdue University in West Lafayette, Indiana.

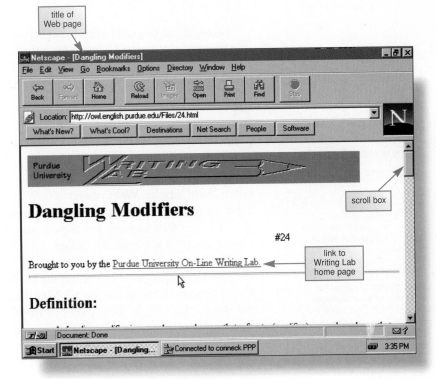

FIGURE 2-45

6 **Scroll down to see examples of proper and improper usage of modifiers.**

Examples of dangling modifiers and revisions display (Figure 2-46). Help with other writing topics is available on the Writing Lab home page.

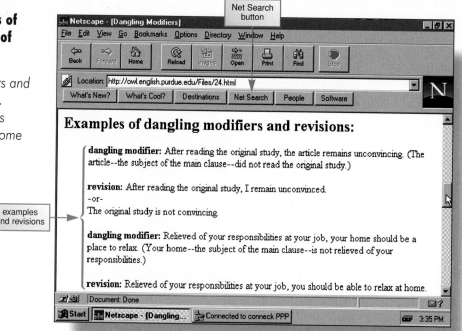

examples and revisions

FIGURE 2-46

Most of the popular search engines allow you to customize the search options in a manner similar to Lycos. You have learned how to set options and search the Web using the Lycos search engine. The last Web search engine, WebCrawler, also searches the contents and titles of Web pages.

Searching the Web Using WebCrawler

Another World Wide Web search tool available on the Net Search Web page is called WebCrawler. **WebCrawler** is a Web search program administered by America Online. WebCrawler uses an automated program that travels around the World Wide Web looking for topics, automatically following links it finds, and adding them to a searchable index.

To illustrate using WebCrawler, you will search for information about one of the new developments happening on the World Wide Web: live 3d and virtual reality modeling language, or VRML. This is the next phase in the evolution of the World Wide Web. Web pages in the future will be 3-dimensional in nature, allowing you to navigate not only up and down the page, but also into the Web page. You will be able to rotate the Web page around in a clockwise fashion. To start the search for live3d sites, display the WebCrawler search page, as shown in the following steps.

Steps **To Display the WebCrawler Page**

① **Click the Net Search directory button to display the Net Search page. Scroll down the Net Search page until the Global Search link displays. Click the Global Search link. Scroll down the Global Search page until the WebCrawler link displays.**

Links to other Web search engines display (Figure 2-47). A brief explanation of the search engine follows each link.

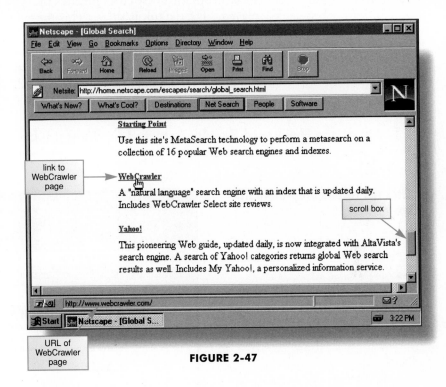

FIGURE 2-47

② **Click the WebCrawler link.**

The WebCrawler Searching page displays (Figure 2-48). This page contains several buttons you can click to request services such as add a URL, browse through random links, and request help. There are two drop-down list boxes where search options can be set. Next there is a text box for entering keywords and a Search button to initiate the search.

FIGURE 2-48

Like AltaVista, InfoSeek, and Lycos, WebCrawler has a text box where you enter keywords and a Search button to start the search. The Search the web and show drop-down list box indicates the way the results of the search will be displayed. The default is titles. This means only the titles of the Web pages will be displayed in the results.

Notice the for results drop-down list box where you can control how many URLs of Web pages containing your keywords to return. The default is 25. You can adjust the number of results returned, as shown in the following steps.

Steps To Adjust the Number of Results Returned by WebCrawler

1 **Click the results drop-down list box arrow.**

A drop-down list box displays with a list of suggested numbers (Figure 2-49).

2 **Click 100 in the drop-down list box.**

The box disappears, and the number 100 displays in the for results drop-down list box.

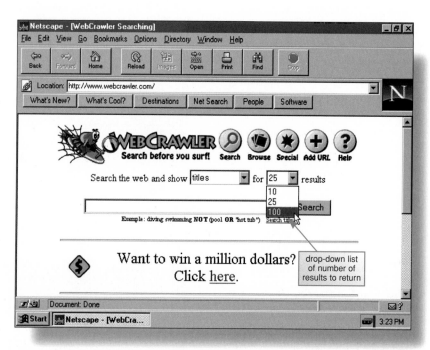

FIGURE 2-49

Some searches can return thousands of URLs, so limiting the number to return can reduce the amount of links you have to look through. You might also want to increase the number of hits displayed so the number of pages you have to load is reduced.

You must select one of the numbers in the box. Having set the number of URLs to return, you can now perform the search. Because you are interested in live3d, that word would be good to use as the keyword for this search.

Steps **To Perform a Web Search Using WebCrawler**

1 **Click the text box to display an insertion point. Type** live3d **in the text box. Point to the Search button.**

The keyword live3d displays in the text box (Figure 2-50).

FIGURE 2-50

2 **Click the Search button.**

After a brief period of time, the WebCrawler Search Results page displays (Figure 2-51). The time required for the search depends on the number selected in the for results drop-down list box. The page contains 100 out of 155 hits.

FIGURE 2-51

3 **Scroll down to reveal the titles of the Web pages containing the live3d keyword.**

The titles of Web pages containing the keyword live3d display (Figure 2-52). Each title is preceded by an oblong bullet. There is a page titled VRML and Live 3D that looks like it would contain information about this new feature.

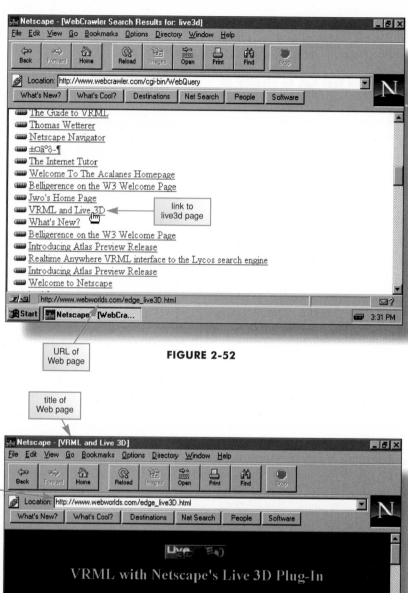

FIGURE 2-52

4 **Click the VRML and Live3D link.**

The VRML and Live3D Web page displays (Figure 2-53). The URL for the Web page displays in the location text box.

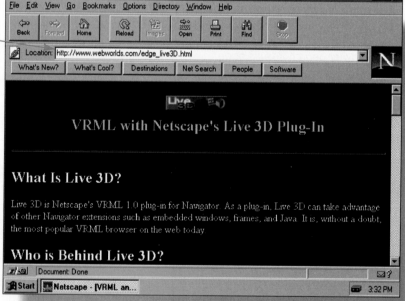

FIGURE 2-53

5 **Scroll down the page to reveal a sample 3-dimensional image.**

A 3-dimensional picture displays (Figure 2-54). There is a small table inside the building. Because this is a 3-dimensional image, you can navigate around within it using the mouse buttons and mouse movement. You can drag the image away or toward you using the left mouse button. You can rotate the image clockwise or counter-clockwise by right-dragging the image using the corresponding circular motion.

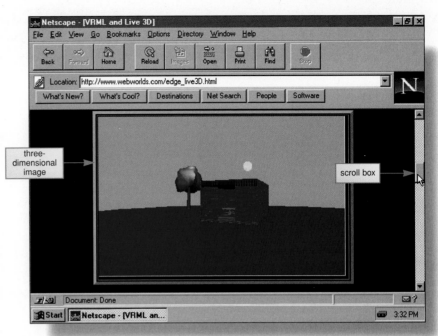

FIGURE 2-54

6 **Move the image by pointing to the image and dragging or right-dragging.**

The picture moves based on which mouse button was held and which direction the mouse is moved (Figure 2-55). There is a pop-up menu of navigation and other commands related to 3-dimensional image management that will display by right-clicking the 3D image. You can return to the WebCrawler page and choose another VRML page to display.

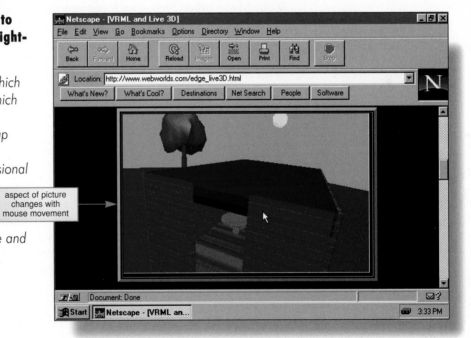

FIGURE 2-55

You have learned how to search the World Wide Web using five of the more popular Web search engines: the Yahoo Directory, Infoseek, AltaVista, Lycos, and WebCrawler. Table 2-1 summarizes these search engines and the search methods used.

More *About*
Search Engines

With the Web growing so rapidly every day, no search engine can index all the available resources. However, most people pick one favorite search engine and use that one exclusively, creating a bookmark to speed access to the search engine.

TABLE 2-1	
SEARCH TOOL	*SEARCH METHOD*
Yahoo Directory	Traverses topic-based menus. Pages submitted by authors for inclusion in menus.
Infoseek	Searches database of computerized periodicals, FTP, gopher, USENET news groups, 19,000,000+ Web pages. Database maintained by Infoseek Corporation.
AltaVista	Searches index of newsgroups and more than 60 million Web pages. Automated program travels around Web finding pages.
WebCrawler	Searches index of Web pages. Automated program travels around Web finding pages.
Lycos	Searches a database of more than 30 million URLs.

The search tools discussed in Table 2-1 are the more popular ones used on the Web. Many other Web search engines are available.

Although search engines such as those in Table 2-1 above help you sort through the millions of Web pages available on the World Wide Web, many more files and programs are available on the Internet that are not part of the World Wide Web. The following section introduces you to a way to access these files and programs using an Internet service called FTP.

Retrieving Files with FTP

The second most popular activity on the Internet, after electronic mail, is transferring files. With FTP, you can retrieve software, data files, word processing documents, graphics, pictures, movies, and sound clips.

The program that assists in this activity is called **FTP**, or **File Transfer Protocol**, which moves files between different computer systems. FTP has a set of commands used to transfer files and perform file management tasks. When using FTP within Netscape, however, no commands are necessary. You use the point and click method, similarly to following hypertext links.

Unfortunately, you do have to know the URL of the computer where these files are located. Using the many well-known FTP sites, called **repositories**, or **FTP archives**, you can access a variety of interesting programs and files stored for public access. As you gain experience with the Internet, you will discover more FTP sites for which you can create bookmarks. See page NN 1.24 in Project 1 for information on creating bookmarks.

To illustrate using FTP in Netscape, you will connect to ftp.netscape.com, Netscape Communications Corporation's FTP site, and obtain the latest release of Netscape for Windows 95. The following steps show how to establish an FTP session in Netscape to Netscape Communications Corporation's FTP computer.

Steps **To Connect to an FTP Site**

1 **Click the location text box.**

The URL is highlighted (Figure 2-56).

URL highlighted

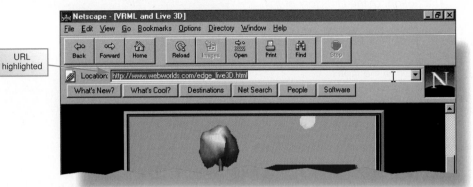

FIGURE 2-56

2 **Type** `ftp://ftp.netscape.com` **in the location text box.**

The new FTP URL replaces the live3D URL (Figure 2-57). Notice the protocol in the URL has changed from http to ftp.

URL of FTP site

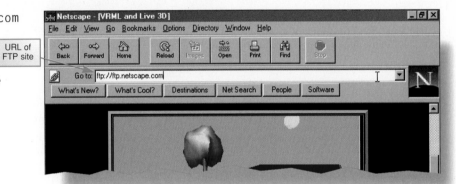

FIGURE 2-57

title of Web page

3 **Press the ENTER key.**

The Directory of / Web page displays (Figure 2-58). The name of the current folder (directory) is shown, followed by information about the FTP site. Links to files and folders available at the FTP site are located toward the bottom of the page.

Current directory is /

information about FTP site

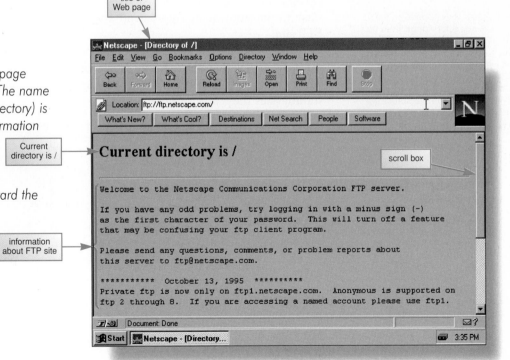

FIGURE 2-58

4 **Scroll down until the pub folder displays.**

The bottom of the Directory of / Web page displays (Figure 2-59). The icons on the left represent folders. The names of the folders display next to the icons.

icons represent directories

URL of pub directory

FIGURE 2-59

When connecting to an FTP site using Netscape, the page in the display area will contain a listing of all the files and folders that are stored in the current folder (directory). Most FTP sites are divided into folders, providing smaller, more manageable lists of files than if all the files on the disk displayed in one long list.

You can move around the folder structure by clicking folder links in the current folder (directory) page. The **current folder (directory)** is the disk folder in the site's directory structure that is shown in the Web page. The name of the current folder (directory) is displayed in the title bar of the Netscape window. The slash in the title bar in Figure 2-59 above indicates the **root folder (directory)** of the FTP site.

Notice in Figure 2-59 the pictures, or icons, next to the filenames. The icons that can be displayed in a folder represent different types of files and indicate what will happen when the link that identifies that file is clicked. Table 2-2 summarizes the icons and their meanings.

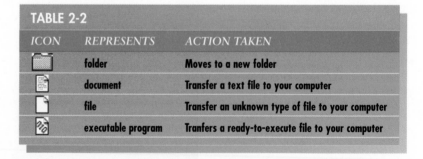

ICON	REPRESENTS	ACTION TAKEN
	folder	Moves to a new folder
	document	Transfer a text file to your computer
	file	Transfer an unknown type of file to your computer
	executable program	Tranfers a ready-to-execute file to your computer

TABLE 2-2

Navigating through Public Access FTP Folders (Directories)

Most FTP sites organize their files into folders using some type of classification. Files can be organized by computer operating system such as MSDOS or UNIX or by general software topics such as graphics or utilities. The starting folder for public access is traditionally called **pub**, which is the second link from the bottom in Figure 2-59.

Netscape lets you access files with FTP in the same way you access World Wide Web pages. However, you may find the FTP pages have minimal formatting. Netscape shows only the type, size, date and a short description of each file in a directory. The following steps show how to navigate through the public access FTP folders.

 Steps To Navigate through Public Access FTP Folders

1 Click the pub link.

The Directory of /pub Web page displays (Figure 2-60). The folder (directory) contains eleven links. The first returns you to the previous folder. The next ten point to folders with software indicated by the folder's name.

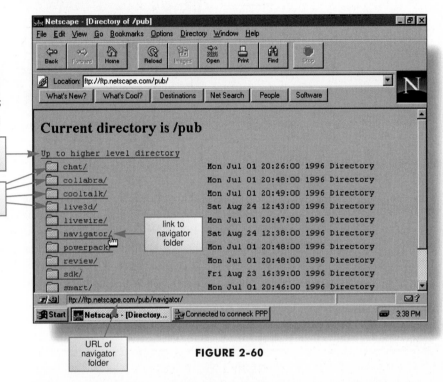

link to previous folder

folders organized by software category

link to navigator folder

URL of navigator folder

FIGURE 2-60

2 Click the navigator link.

Links to directories containing different versions of Netscape Navigator display (Figure 2-61). The 3.0 link contains the most recent version of Netscape. Notice how the files at this FTP site are organized by title, then version. You can continue to maneuver through the folder structure by clicking folder links.

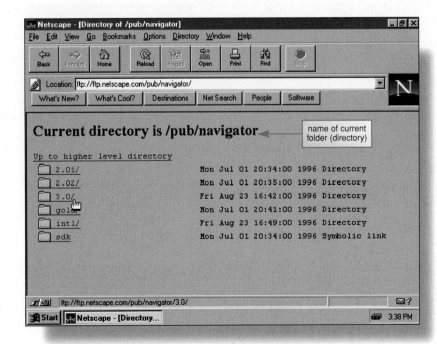

name of current folder (directory)

FIGURE 2-61

3 **Click the 3.0 link. Click the windows link. Scroll down the page.**

Links to the Netscape files display (Figure 2-62).

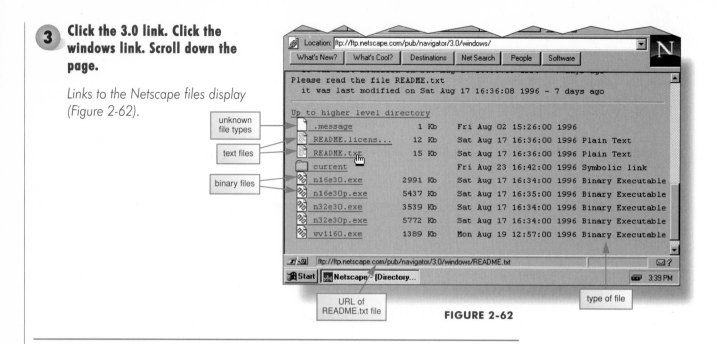

unknown file types

text files

binary files

URL of README.txt file

type of file

FIGURE 2-62

Notice that this Web page includes several files. The first two files contain information about obtaining a license for the Netscape product. The last five are labeled Binary Executable files. These files contain copies of the Netscape program. The README.txt file contains information about which of the binary executable files will work with Windows 95. To see what the README.txt file contains, you must first retrieve it, as shown in the following steps.

To Retrieve Files Using FTP

1 **Click the README.txt link.**

The contents of the README.txt file display (Figure 2-63). Instructions directing you to read and understand the license for using Netscape display at the beginning of the page.

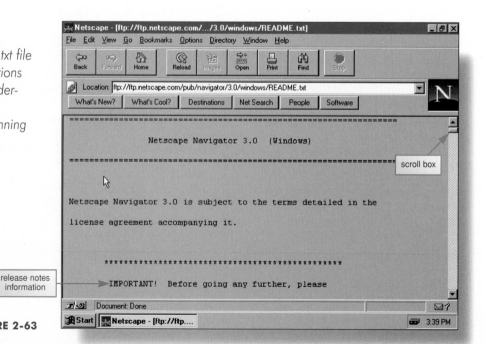

scroll box

release notes information

FIGURE 2-63

2 **Scroll down the page to reveal the installation instructions.**

Information displays describing which binary executable file (the 32-bit version) should be downloaded for use with Windows 95 (Figure 2-64). Most public access FTP sites have a readme file or an index text file that contains information about the files stored there. You can now return to the windows folder to retrieve the executable file.

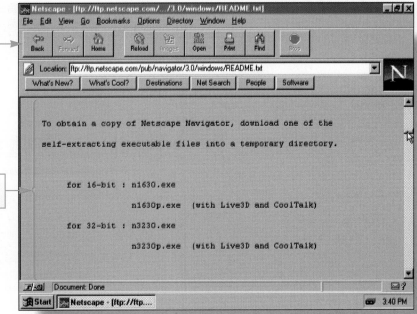

FIGURE 2-64

3 **Click the Back button on the Netscape toolbar.**

The Directory of /pub/navigator/3.0/windows Web page redisplays (Figure 2-65). The n32e30p.exe link is the 32-bit version of Netscape. This is the version that will run with Windows 95. The file is more than 5 million bytes in size. The n16e30p.exe link is the 16-bit version of Netscape. This version will run with Windows 3.x.

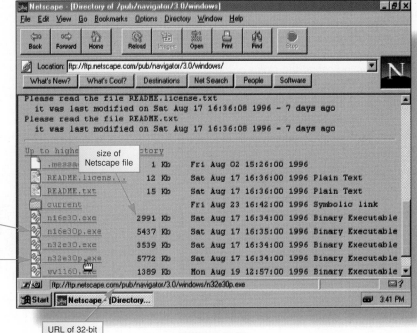

FIGURE 2-65

4 **Click the n32e30p.exe link.**

The Save As dialog box displays with n32e30p as the default filename (Figure 2-66). The file is too large to store on a floppy disk, so it must be written to a folder on the hard drive. The default hard drive letter may be different on your computer. If you do not know which drive letter to use, ask your instructor for the proper drive letter.

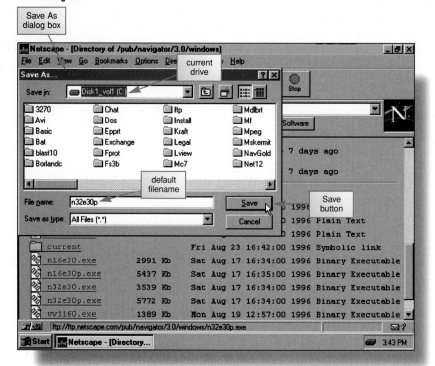

FIGURE 2-66

5 **Click the Save button to accept n32e30p.exe as the filename.**

The Saving Location dialog box displays indicating the status of the transfer (Figure 2-67). When the transfer is complete, the Saving Location dialog box disappears.

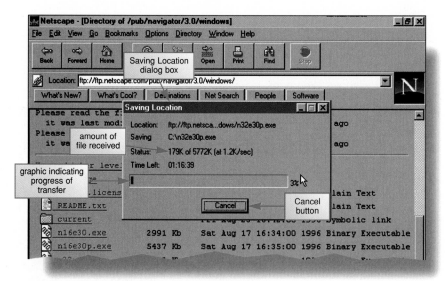

FIGURE 2-67

More *About* **File Transfer**

If you perform frequent file transfer to and from your personal computer, it may be wise to create a file transfer folder as a staging area. Then all the files you download from other sites would go to this folder, simplifying management of the files.

If for some reason you wanted to stop the transfer, you would click the Cancel button in the Saving Location dialog box. You have successfully retrieved the latest version of the Netscape Web browser program.

You might want to create a bookmark to the ftp site, so you can retrieve new versions of Netscape as they become available. Refer to the section on creating bookmarks in Project 1 on page NN 1.24.

Other files and programs, such as the NetChat program, which is used for conversing over the Internet, can be retrieved in the same manner, as shown in the following steps.

Retrieving a Copy of NetChat

NetChat, which is a program that allows you to talk to other people over the Internet, will be discussed in Project 3. You can obtain a copy now, in preparation for use in the next project. The following steps retrieve a copy of the NetChat program.

 Steps To Obtain a Copy of NetChat

1 **Click the Back button on the toolbar until the Directory of /pub Web page redisplays.**

The Directory of /pub Web page displays (Figure 2-68). The chat folder contains files associated with NetChat.

Back button

current folder is pub

link to NetChat software

FIGURE 2-68

2 **Click the chat/ link. Click the windows link. Scroll down the page.**

The Directory of /pub/chat/windows Web page displays (Figure 2-69). The page contains six links. Just as Netscape includes 16- and 32-bit versions, 16- and 32-bit versions of NetChat also are available. The 32-bit version is the one used for Windows 95.

link to 32-bit NetChat

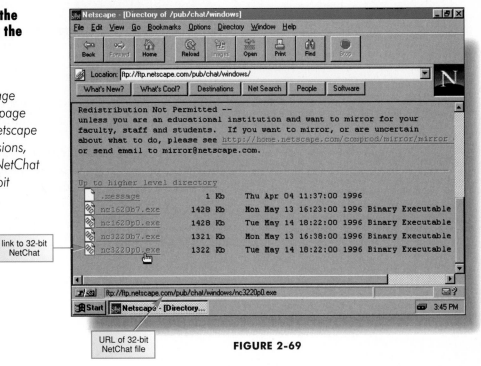

URL of 32-bit NetChat file

FIGURE 2-69

3 Click the nc3220p0.exe link.

The Save As dialog box displays with nc3220p0 as the default filename (Figure 2-70). The default drive may be different on your computer. If you do not know which drive letter to use, ask your instructor for the proper drive letter.

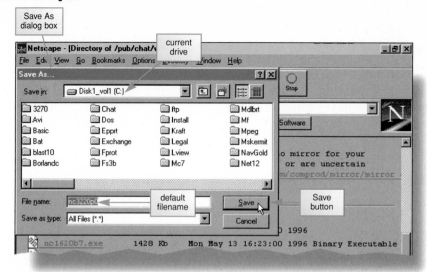

FIGURE 2-70

4 Click the Save button to save nc3220p0.exe to the hard drive.

The Saving Location dialog box displays indicating the status of the transfer (Figure 2-71). When the transfer is complete, the Saving Location dialog box disappears.

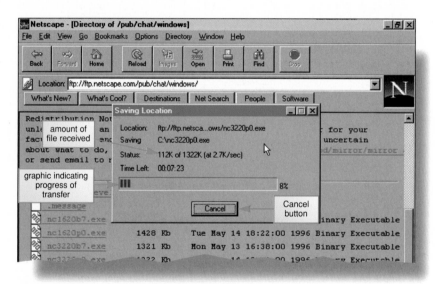

FIGURE 2-71

More *About* Obtaining Programs with FTP

Netscape uses other programs, called helper applications, to take advantage of different types of multimedia and other computer facilities. You can use search engines to find out about the numerous helper applications available, and then use FTP to download them for use with Netscape.

You have learned how to retrieve files using FTP. Thousands of other FTP sites exist for you to explore. Appendix A contains several popular and useful public access FTP sites.

FTP is one of the service programs that was part of the Internet long before the World Wide Web. Another Internet service program that pre-dates the World Wide Web but is still very useful, is called gopher.

Using Gopher to Retrieve Files

Initially developed at the University of Minnesota to help its users find answers to local computing questions, **gopher** has since developed into a worldwide service that helps organize the vast collection of information available on the Internet.

Gopher started out as a document retrieval system. Over time, it has been modified to serve as a user-friendly, menu-driven method of retrieving files. When using gopher, you are presented with a list of menu commands much like FTP. Clicking one of the commands might display another menu of commands, or retrieve a file and store it on your computer.

You access a gopher site the same way you access an FTP site, by supplying a URL that Netscape can use to connect to the gopher site. The following steps show how to connect to the gopher at Cornell Law School at Ithaca, New York, and display information about the Americans With Disabilities Act.

Steps **To Start a Gopher Session**

1 **Click the location text box to highlight the URL. Type** gopher://fatty.law.cornell .edu **in the text box.**

The FTP URL disappears when the new URL is typed (Figure 2-72). Notice the URL protocol is now gopher.

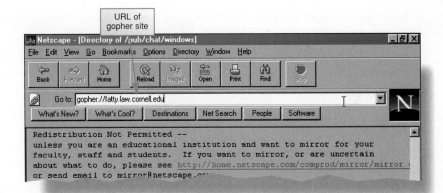

FIGURE 2-72

2 **Press the ENTER key.**

The Gopher Menu page displays (Figure 2-73). The icons and associated links represent lower-level gopher menus, each containing several links. Legal areas such as Foreign, International, and U.S. Law are available.

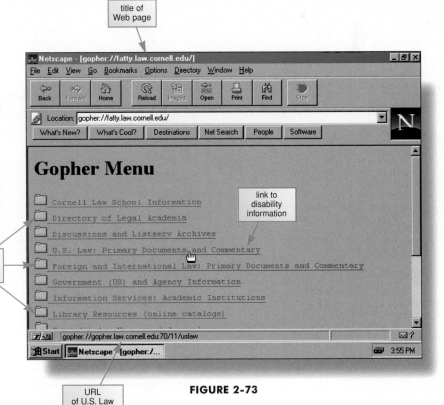

FIGURE 2-73

Navigating Gopher Menus

The layout of the gopher menus is similar to the FTP directory pages discussed earlier. Links to other menu items are identified by the same icons used with FTP (see Table 2-2 on page NN 2.36). To navigate through the gopher menus to find data about the Americans With Disabilities Act, start by clicking the U.S. Law: Primary Documents and Commentary link, as shown in the following steps.

Steps **To Navigate Gopher Menus**

1 **Click the U.S. Law: Primary Documents and Commentary link in the column of links under the Gopher Menu.**

The uslaw Web page displays (Figure 2-74). This page includes links to documents describing such things as Copyright, Patent, and Trade-mark law, as well as the Americans With Disabilities Act.

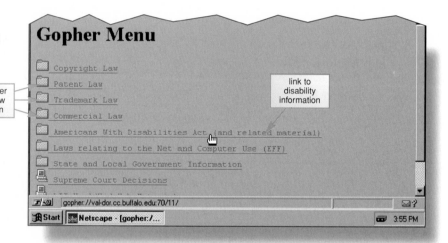

FIGURE 2-74

2 **Click the Americans With Disabilities Act link.**

*Another Gopher Menu page displays (Figure 2-75). Notice the URL in the location text box is val-dor.cc.buffalo.edu. You have left the Cornell gopher and have connected to a gopher at the State University of New York at Buffalo, New York. This demonstrates that gophers can be linked together. This interconnected collection of gophers is called **gopherspace**. Interesting facts about disabilities can be found in the Statistics link.*

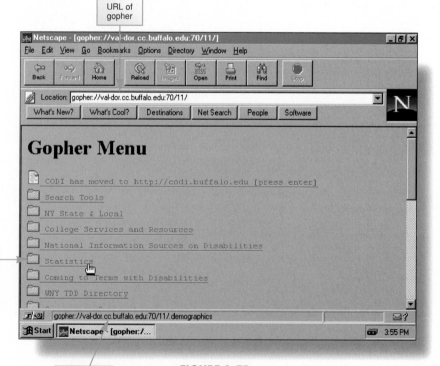

FIGURE 2-75

3 **Click the Statistics link.**

The demographics Web page displays (Figure 2-76). Links to five documents and one directory are available on the page. Statistics about disabilities are found in the Disability Statistics link.

link to Disability Statistics

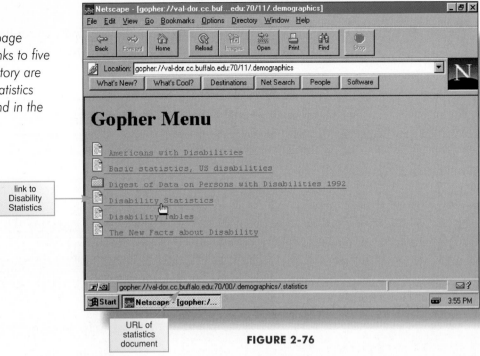

URL of statistics document

FIGURE 2-76

4 **Click the Disability Statistics link.**

Statistics about disabilities display (Figure 2-77). Scroll through the page to see statistics on different types of disabilities.

information about blind persons

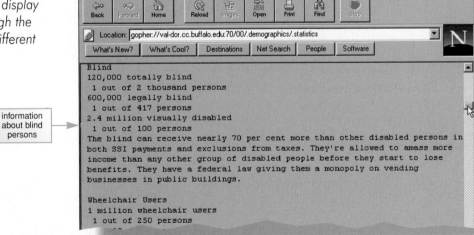

FIGURE 2-77

You can see that 1 in 2,000 persons are totally blind. Following the statistics for blindness are statistics on wheelchair usage. The displayed page can now be printed or saved on a floppy disk.

If you want to study other disability information, you can move back to the previous gopher menus by clicking the Back button on the Netscape toolbar. Just as there are many public access FTP sites, there are many public access gopher sites you can contact. See Appendix A for the locations of other interesting gopher sites.

More *About* **Gopher**

Gopher is used extensively by federal, state and local government agencies as a means for making available information, copies of forms and documents, and other government services. You can use search engines to find out the URL of a particular government agency and browse through their site. You will most likely find one of several gophers there.

Exiting Netscape

When you are finished transferring files, you follow the steps discussed in Project 1 to exit Netscape. This step is summarized below.

TO EXIT NETSCAPE

Step 1: Click the Close button (Figure 2-78).

The Windows 95 desktop displays.

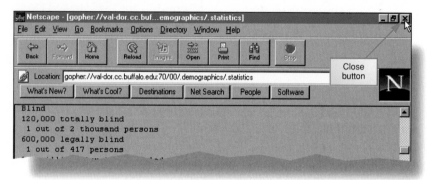

FIGURE 2-78

Project Summary

After completing Project 2, you now have enough knowledge about Web search engines to be able to assist library patrons in their search for information on the World Wide Web. In this project, you learned how to search the World Wide Web using the Yahoo Directory. Setting search and display options and entering keywords was demonstrated for the Infoseek, AltaVista, Lycos, and WebCrawler search engines. You also learned how to retrieve files with FTP and gopher.

What You Should Know

Having completed the project, you now should be able to perform the following tasks:

▶ Access Web Search Tools *(NN 2.6)*
▶ Adjust the Number of Results Returned by WebCrawler *(NN 2.30)*
▶ Connect to an FTP Site *(NN 2.35)*
▶ Display the AltaVista Web Page *(NN 2.18)*
▶ Display the Lycos Search Form *(NN 2.23)*
▶ Display the Lycos Search Options Form *(NN 2.24)*
▶ Display the Next Set of Infoseek Search Results *(NN 2.16)*
▶ Display the WebCrawler Page *(NN 2.29)*
▶ Display the Yahoo Directory Web Page *(NN 2.7)*
▶ Exit Netscape *(NN 2.46)*

▶ Navigate Gopher Menus *(NN 2.44)*
▶ Navigate through Public Access FTP Folders *(NN 2.37)*
▶ Obtain a Copy of NetChat *(NN 2.41)*
▶ Perform a Web Search Using Infoseek *(NN 2.12)*
▶ Perform a Search Using Lycos *(NN 2.26)*
▶ Perform a Web Search Using WebCrawler *(NN 2.31)*
▶ Perform a Web Search Using the Yahoo Directory *(NN 2.8)*
▶ Retrieve Files Using FTP *(NN 2.38)*
▶ Search the Web Using AltaVista *(NN 2.19)*
▶ Start a Gopher Session *(NN 2.43)*
▶ Start Netscape *(NN 2.5)*

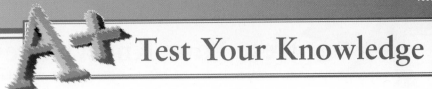

Test Your Knowledge

1 True/False

Instructions: Circle T if the statement is true or F if the statement is false.

T F 1. Web search tools allow you to search in terms of where a file is located.

T F 2. The Yahoo Directory is accessed by clicking the Internet Directory button.

T F 3. WebCrawler uses a series of menus to organize links to Web pages.

T F 4. AltaVista has more than 18 million Web pages in it's index.

T F 5. With most Web search engines, when you type more than one keyword in the text box, you can control whether both must appear in the Web page or whether one or the other must appear in the Web page.

T F 6. WebCrawler search results include a relevance score.

T F 7. The FTP (File Transfer Protocol) program moves files between computers.

T F 8. The icons on the FTP directory pages identify the types of files found there.

T F 9. Most FTP sites organize their files into directories using some logical technique, such as operating system name or software topic.

T F 10. Gopher menus have icons similar to FTP directory pages.

2 Multiple Choice

Instructions: Circle the correct response.

1. The search engine that allows you to alter the number of URLs returned is _____.
   a. NetChat
   b. Yahoo Directory
   c. gopher
   d. WebCrawler

2. The search engine that uses a list of general categories from which you repeatedly select a topic is called _____.
   a. Eudora
   b. Yahoo Directory
   c. gopher
   d. WebCrawler

3. The letters FTP stand for _____.
   a. File Transfer Protocol
   b. Find the Program
   c. File Transport Program
   d. they do not stand for anything

(continued)

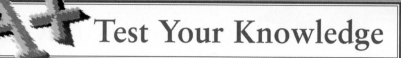

Test Your Knowledge

Multiple Choice *(continued)*

4. The name of that portion of the disk where the user is located in an FTP site's directory structure is called _____.
   a. a Web page
   b. the URL
   c. the thread
   d. the current directory

5. The collection of interconnected gophers is called _____.
   a. Yahoo
   b. gopherspace
   c. FTP archive
   d. the Internet

6. Access to Yahoo is achieved by clicking the _____ button.
   a. Net Search
   b. Newsgroups
   c. Back
   d. Net Directory

7. _____ are the word(s) you enter that are used by the search engine to search the Web.
   a. Option buttons
   b. Icons
   c. Keywords
   d. URLs

8. The special score or percentage associated with each match returned is called a _____.
   a. relevance score
   b. hit
   c. link
   d. keyword

9. Having to alter the keywords to exclude unrelated Web pages is called _____ the search.
   a. abandoning
   b. refining
   c. performing
   d. re-running

10. A smaller version of a larger picture used to save transfer time and page space is called a(n) _____ picture.
    a. smaller
    b. icon
    c. thumbnail
    d. sample

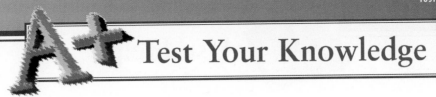

Test Your Knowledge

3 Understanding the Lycos Advanced Search Options

Instructions: In Figure 2-79, arrows point to several areas of the Lycos Search Form Web page. Identify the various parts of the page in the spaces provided.

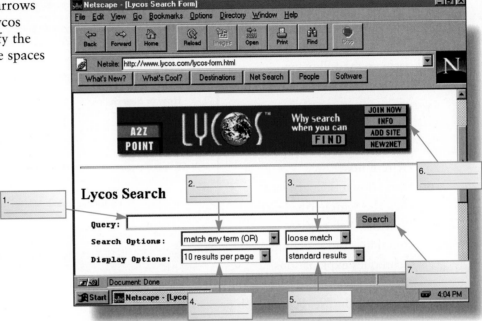

FIGURE 2-79

4 Understanding the AltaVista Web Page

Instructions: In Figure 2-80, arrows point to several areas of the AltaVista: Main Page Web page. Identify the various parts of the page in the spaces provided.

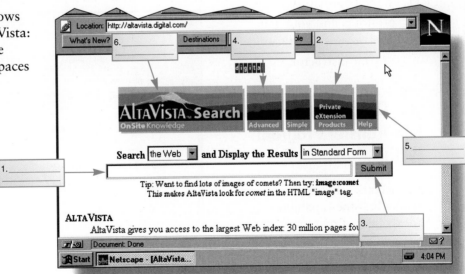

FIGURE 2-80

Use Help

1 Obtaining Help for Web Search Tools

Instructions: Start Netscape and perform the following tasks with a computer:

1. Click the Net Search button.
2. Click the INFOSEEK GUIDE link.
3. Scroll down the page and click the Search Tips link.
4. Print the Web page containing the searching techniques explanations (Figure 2-81).
5. Return to the Net Search Web page.
6. Scroll down to and then click the WebCrawler link.
7. Scroll down to the help link at the bottom of the WebCrawler page and click the link.
8. Click the Examples link.
9. Print the Web page containing the searching techniques explanations.
10. Write a brief comparison of Infoseek and WebCrawler search techniques.
11. Write your name on the printouts and your comparison and turn them in to your instructor.

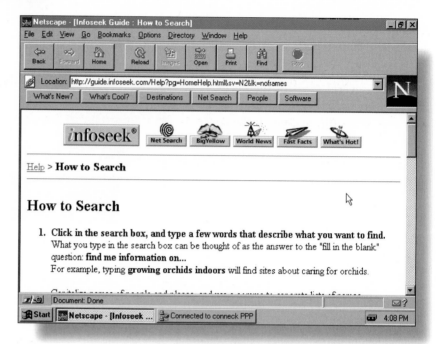

FIGURE 2-81

2 Obtaining Help for File Transfer Program (FTP)

Instructions: Retrieving files is only half the capabilities of File Transfer Program. It is possible to send files to other computers with Netscape. Start Netscape and perform the following tasks with a computer:

FIGURE 2-82

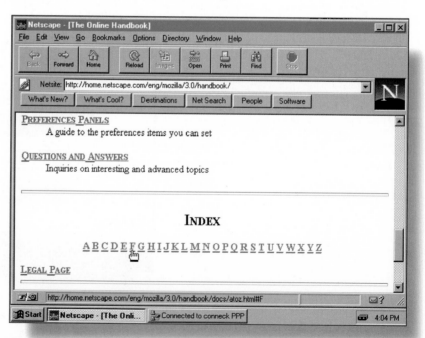

Use Help

1. Click Handbook on the Help menu to display Netscape help.
2. Scroll down to the alphabetical index at the bottom of the form and click the F link (Figure 2-82).
3. Scroll down to reveal the links to FTP help information. Click the Sending and Retrieving files link.
4. Display the information about how to send files to another computer using Netscape.
5. Write a brief explanation of how to send files using FTP with Netscape and turn it in to your instructor.
6. Optional - If you have access to another computer account, try sending a file from a PC using Netscape to your other computer account. What, if any problems did you encounter? Include a description of your experience in the brief explanation in step 5.

In the Lab

1 Searching the Web with Infoseek

Instructions: Start Netscape and perform the following tasks with a computer:

1. Select the following topics one at a time: geology, motorcycle, fungus, molecule, tiddlywinks, and shark.
2. Using Infoseek, perform a search on the topic.
3. Select one of the links returned and follow it until you find a picture of your topic (Figure 2-83).
4. Print a picture for each topic, write your name on it and turn it in to your instructor.

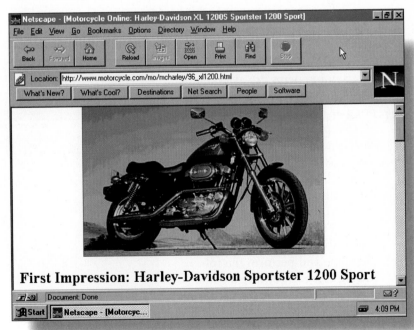

FIGURE 2-83

In the Lab

2 Searching the Web with WebCrawler

Instructions: Start Netscape and perform the following tasks with a computer:

1. Select the following topics one at a time: gorilla, football, cloud, rock, engine, baby.
2. Using WebCrawler, perform a search on the topic.
3. Select one of the links returned and follow it until you find a picture of your topic (Figure 2-84).
4. Print a picture for each topic, write your name on it and turn it in to your instructor.

FIGURE 2-84

3 Retrieving a File Using FTP

Instructions: Thousands of entertaining items are available on the Internet. One of the more popular items is computer games. Several public access FTP sites exist where numerous games are stored. Most of the games are in a special compressed format called **zipped**. This saves disk space. You need an unzip program to uncompress the game in preparation for installing it. Start Netscape and perform the following tasks to retrieve a game and the unzip program:

1. Using FTP, connect to ftp.cdrom.com.

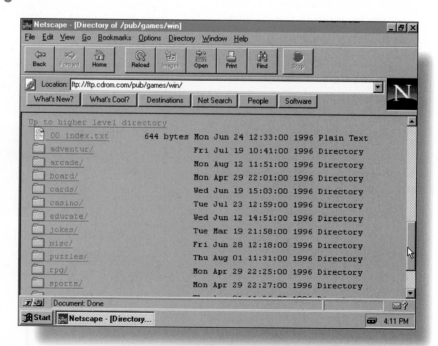

FIGURE 2-85

In the Lab

2. Move to the /pub/games/win directory. You will see directories containing categories of games (Figure 2-85).
3. Choose one of the game categories, and display the 00_index.txt file in that directory.
4. Read through the index until you see a game you like.
5. Print the page containing the explanation of your game.
6. Return to the previous Web page using the Back button.
7. Scroll down the page and retrieve the file containing the game.
8. Move to the /pub/simtel/win3 directory.
9. Retrieve the unzip.exe program.
10. To use the unzip program to uncompress the game, type `unzip name-of-game-file` at the MSDOS prompt. (Substitute the actual filename of your game for name-of-game-file.)
11. Follow the instructions for installing the game that are contained in the readme file included along with the game.
12. Play the game and write a brief review of the game.
13. Write your name on the printout generated in Step 5, along with the review of the game, and turn it in to your instructor.

4 Retrieving Files Using Gopher

Instructions: Start Netscape and perform the following tasks with a computer:

1. Connect to gopher://gopher.nara.gov.
2. Click Information about NARA holdings.
3. Click Information about records retained by Washington DC area repositories.
4. Click Audiovisual records.
5. Click Still Pictures.
6. Click Pictures of the Civil War [the photos].
7. Select one of the pictures to display (Figure 2-86).
8. Print the picture, write your name on the output and turn it in to your instructor.

FIGURE 2-86

In the Lab

5 Searching the Web Using Yahoo

Instructions: Start Netscape and perform the following tasks with a computer:

1. Click the Net Search button and scroll down to reveal the YAHOO! link.
2. Click the link to display the Yahoo Directory.
3. Under the Computers:Internet:World Wide Web category, find and display a Virtual Reality Modeling Language (VRML) 3-dimensional image (Figure 2-87).
4. Using Help, find out what the commands (walk, spin, etc.) at the bottom of the display area are for.
5. Write a brief description of the commands, along with when you might use them, and turn it in to your instructor.

FIGURE 2-87

In the Lab

6 Setting Lycos Search Options

Instructions: Start Netscape and perform the following tasks with a computer:

1. Display the Lycos advanced search options Web page.
2. Search for the keyword, gold.
3. Print the page containing the results. Write your name on the printout.
4. On the Lycos Search Form, change the search options from loose match to strong match (Figure 2-88).
5. Perform the search again for the keyword, gold. Why are the results so different?
6. Print the page containing the results. Write your name on the printout.

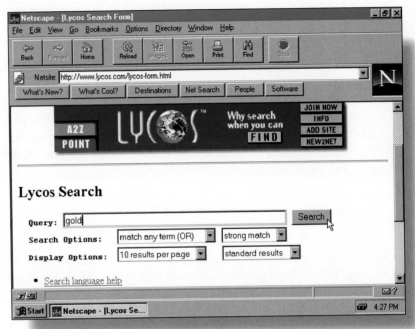

FIGURE 2-88

7. Write your answer on the back of one of the printouts and turn both printouts in to your instructor.

Cases and Places

The difficulty of these case studies varies:

▶ Case studies preceded by a single half moon are the least difficult. You are asked to perform the exercise based on techniques learned in the project.

▶▶ Case studies preceded by two half moons are more difficult. You must perform the exercise and carry out calculations.

▶▶▶ Case studies preceded by three half moons are the most difficult. You must perform the exercise by obtaining and organizing the necessary information and then prepare a report.

Cases and Places

1 ▶ During one of the Rolling Stones last world tours, the Rolling Stones Web page was one of the most popular pages on the World Wide Web, accumulating hundreds of thousands of visits. The Stones are not the only group with home pages on the Web. Using the search engine of your choice, find out when and where your favorite performer, band, or rock group will be playing next. Find and print the home page, if one is available.

2 ▶ You have been hired by one of the best restaurants in New York City as its wine steward. You notice the stock of California white wines is getting low. Use at least two different search engines and find three sources from each search engine for a fruity California white wine. Compare the prices for the wine, prices for shipping, and when the wine will be available.

3 ▶▶ You have been appointed to the town board of zoning appeals. You are the only one with computer experience, and the other board members rely on you for all computer-related activities, including online research. Compile a list of URLs for federal government computers that provides gopher services that include, but are not limited to, information such as federal housing programs, wetlands, and mining. (Hint: some gopher URLs are intuitive, such as gopher.senate.gov.)

4 ▶▶▶ FTP, one of the basic Internet service programs available well before Netscape and the World Wide Web, is a command-based program. You had to know the commands to establish the FTP connection, identify yourself, navigate directories, and request file transfers. Create a list of available FTP commands and their functions. Which functions does Netscape perform for you when retrieving files?

5 ▶▶▶ FTP allows the transfer of files between computers. When using FTP within Netscape, it is possible to send files to another computer. Use online Help to find out what pieces of information and actions are necessary to allow Netscape to send files to another computer. What would have to be changed or added to enable Netscape to send files to a personal computer account?

6 ▶▶▶ Search tools used on the Internet were available well before the advent of the World Wide Web. Two of these search tools are archie and veronica. Using Web search engines, find out what archie and veronica do. Perform a search using archie and veronica. Write a description of how they work, including a brief explanation of important commands and a sample of the search results.

7 ▶▶▶ Web search engines use different techniques for searching Web resources. If you were designing a search engine, what would you look for when determining whether a Web page successfully matches the keywords? Write a list containing the items you would use for determining a Web page is a successful match for keywords. Include an explanation for each item and turn it in to your instructor.

Netscape Navigator 3

Windows 95

Conversing Over the Internet

Objectives:

You will have mastered the material in this project when you can:

▶ Send and receive electronic mail messages
▶ Perform electronic mail management functions
▶ Create an electronic address book
▶ Read and post newsgroup articles
▶ Perform newsgroup management functions
▶ Subscribe to a newsgroup
▶ Unsubscribe from a newsgroup
▶ Converse over the Web using WebChat
▶ Converse over the Internet using NetChat

The Message Heard *Round* the Internet World

The Internet is the hot spot for modern communication exchanges. Sixteen million homes have computers with modems, and more than half access the Internet an average of seven hours per week. Internet users have personal e-mail addresses that can be used to communicate with 40 million other e-mail users all over the world.

The electronic communication revolution started when the Internet was in its infancy. The scientists who first used the Internet realized they could use their addresses to send and receive personal messages. Hence, e-mail was born.

Today, nearly 80 percent of Internet users communicate with e-mail, and this service is one of the major reasons they became users. They send more than three billion messages each month, which is six times more than two years ago and greater than the number of conventional *snail mail* letters sent through the U.S. Postal System. Today, e-mail, newsgroups, and chat rooms abound on the Internet and remain the three most popular methods of Internet communications.

Newsgroups are used by people who share common interests. Nearly one-half of Internet users participate in newsgroups to send their thoughts and opinions about specific topics to other participants. Many people are electronic spectators in newsgroups, reading articles and responses but refraining from sending messages of their own. Newsgroups generally are grouped into several major categories, from science to business and just about everything in between.

Chat rooms, like newsgroups, allow users to enter and participate in live conversations with other people on the Internet. This method of communicating is much like a computerized party line, but users need not dial the 900 prefix or pay $4.95 a minute to join. Some chat rooms are organized around a common theme, set of beliefs, or shared views. For example, users supporting a particular political party can enter a chat room to talk to people who share (or oppose) this view. While some chat rooms are more generic, many are used by people with common ideas.

In short, virtually any forum and subject about which you want to communicate is on the Internet. With a few clicks of the mouse, a cancer patient can find solace and support from others facing the same obstacles. Gardeners can exchange planting tips and information and compare notes with other gardeners. Whatever your intrest, you will find it on the Net.

The Internet provides totally uncensored and unrestricted access to everyone with no background check or psychological test. It is, therefore, wise to be circumspect, if not downright suspicious, while communicating on the Internet, whether through e-mail, a newsgroup, or a chat room. Sensitive information such as a credit card number or personal information such as a name or address should be transmitted cautiously. Recent cases of stalking and credit card scams have illustrated in a painfully clear fashion just how careful one should be. On the upside, though, countless friendships have been forged, priceless comfort and support have been given, and untold knowledge gleaned, all through Internet communications.

Netscape Navigator 3

Windows 95

Conversing Over the Internet

Introduction

Projects 1 and 2 revealed techniques for finding and obtaining information and files using Netscape. Transferring files and information over the World Wide Web is only part of the communications capabilities available. Project 3 continues with a discussion of Web services that allow people from all over the world with similar interests to get together electronically and share their thoughts and opinions on thousands of topics. The services are electronic mail, newsgroups, WebChat, and NetChat.

Electronic Mail

The most popular service on the Internet is **electronic mail,** or **e-mail.** Using e-mail, you can converse with friends across the room or on another continent. If someone you know has an account on America Online, CompuServe, The Microsoft Network (MSN), or an account on a computer connected to the Internet, you can send him or her electronic mail.

Corresponding with electronic mail consists of composing and sending messages to others and managing the messages that others send to you. Netscape is a marvelous tool for using Internet services, including composing, sending, and reading electronic mail messages.

Preparing to Use Netscape for Electronic Mail

Before sending a mail message over the Internet, you must know the recipient's electronic mail address. An individual's **electronic mail address** consists of an account name followed by the @ character, then the Internet address (or domain name) of the remote computer where the person's account is located (Figure 3-1).

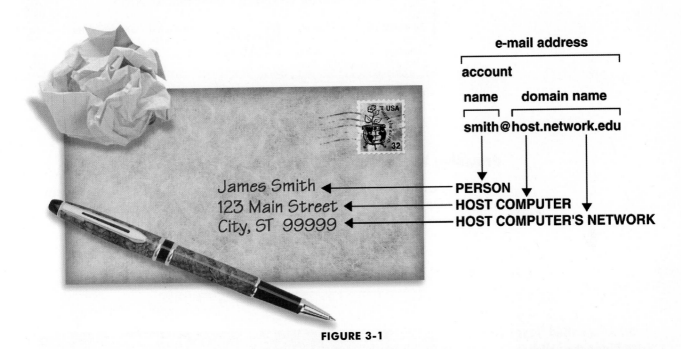

FIGURE 3-1

In addition, you must provide information such as your electronic mail address and your Internet account name to Netscape before sending or reading mail. This information is needed so Netscape can properly deliver your mail to you. The following steps show how to start Netscape and enter the necessary information in the Netscape forms.

Starting Netscape

To start Netscape, follow the procedure you used at the beginning of Project 1 on page NN 1.11. This step is summarized below.

TO START NETSCAPE

Step 1: With the Windows 95 desktop active, double-click the Netscape shortcut icon.

The Netscape window with the Netscape home page displays (Figure 3-2 on the next page). The Netscape home page might display differently on your computer because of continuous changes and updates.

More *About* **Electronic Mail Addresses**

Directories of electronic mail addresses are springing up all over the World Wide Web. Look for them on the Net Search page.

FIGURE 3-2

Providing Your E-Mail Information to Netscape

With Netscape running, you can provide your personal e-mail information using the Options menu. The following steps show how to access the electronic mail preferences windows.

 To Provide Your E-Mail Information to Netscape

1 **Insert a formatted floppy disk in drive B and then click Options on the menu bar.**

The Options menu displays (Figure 3-3). From this menu, you can choose commands that allow you to customize the Netscape program.

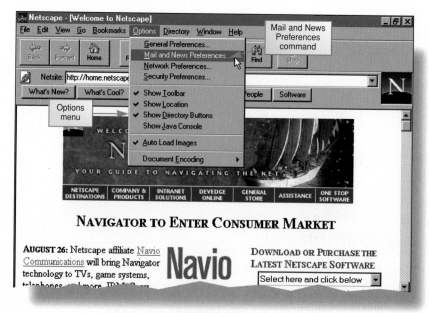

FIGURE 3-3

2 Click **Mail and News Preferences.** Click the **Identity** tab, if necessary.

The Preferences dialog box opens and the Identity sheet displays. In the text boxes, you can enter the information used when sending electronic mail messages (Figure 3-4). Figure 3-4 shows the name of the person sending mail is Kurt Jordan and his electronic mail address is jordank@niia.net.

3 Drag across the name in the **Your Name** text box and then type your full name. Drag across the e-mail address in the **Your Email** text box and then type your e-mail address. If you do not know your e-mail address, ask your instructor. Click the **Servers** tab.

Information about electronic mail and news Internet servers displays (Figure 3-5). The information here tells Netscape where to find the mail that has been sent to you by others. Figure 3-5 shows the address of the computer where mail is stored, the mail account name, and the directory in which to store mail. These entries should reflect your e-mail account.

4 Drag across the name in the **POP3 User Name** text box and then type your Internet mail account name. Do not include the Internet address of the host computer. If you do not know your Internet mail account name, ask your instructor. Drag across the entry in the **Mail Directory** text box and then type **b:** to store any in-coming mail on the floppy disk in drive B. Click the **OK button.**

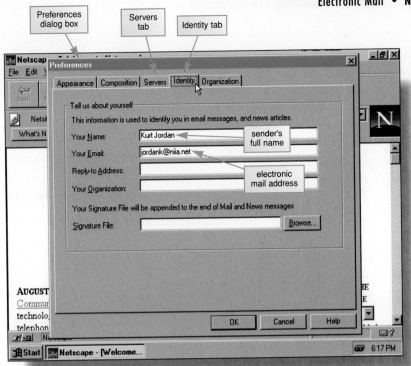

FIGURE 3-4

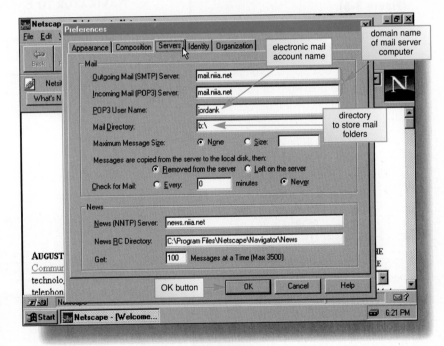

FIGURE 3-5

Other Ways

1. Press ALT+O, press ALT+M

More *About*
E-Mail Preferences

You can instruct Netscape to continuously check for new mail messages every few minutes by changing settings on the Servers sheet.

Your e-mail address will remain in Netscape until you or someone else changes it. This also means that if you are using Netscape in an environment such as a library or college computer laboratory, another user's e-mail address may be stored in the e-mail preferences forms. You will have to change the data to reflect your electronic mail address before using Netscape's e-mail facilities.

Be careful not to change other settings in the Preferences dialog box. Changing any other settings could cause mail and newsgroups not to function.

Accessing Electronic Mail in Netscape

Having supplied your electronic mail information to Netscape, you now can use the electronic mail facilities. Follow these steps to access electronic mail using Netscape.

Steps To Access Electronic Mail Using Netscape

1 Click the mail icon (the small envelope) in the lower right corner of the Netscape window (Figure 3-6).

The Netscape Mail window displays (Figure 3-7). The Password Entry Dialog dialog box opens, prompting you for the password of your electronic mail account that you entered on the Servers sheet in Figure 3-5 on the previous page. The password protects your mail account from access by others. POP3 is the protocol used for transferring electronic mail to and from computers. POP stands for Post Office Protocol. The mail icon indicates the availability of new messages. A question mark (?) adjacent to the envelope indicates Netscape cannot automatically check the status of the mail server. The envelope alone indicates no new messages for you. An exclamation point (!) adjacent to the envelope indicates that new messages are available for retrieval.

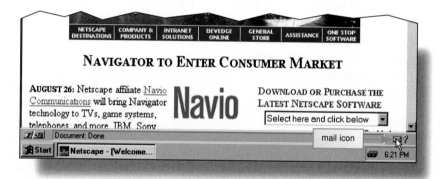

FIGURE 3-6

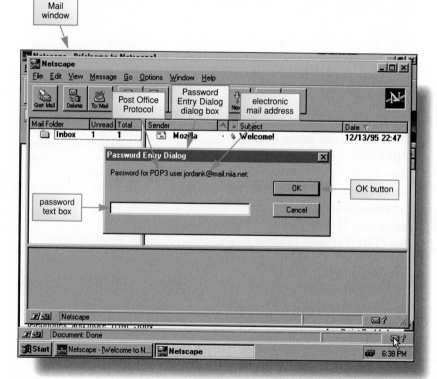

FIGURE 3-7

2 **Type your password. The password will not display in the text box. If you do not know what the password is, ask your instructor for information on how to obtain one.**

Asterisks display in the password text box (Figure 3-8). This ensures no one can see your password as you type it.

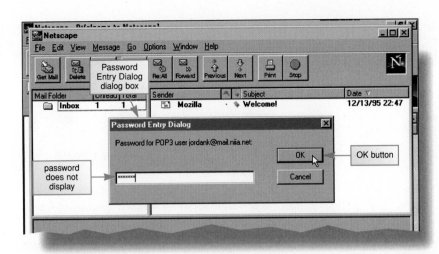

FIGURE 3-8

3 **Click the OK button.**

The Password Entry Dialog dialog box disappears. Netscape will contact the computer containing your mailbox to see if you have any new mail. The Netscape dialog box displays if you have no mail (Figure 3-9). Some computer centers will send a welcome mail message to an account when it is first created. You might see this welcome message on your computer.

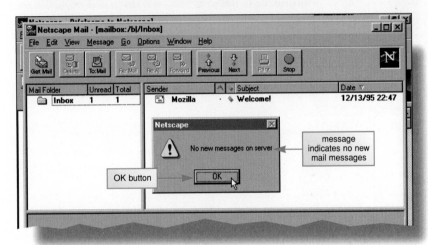

FIGURE 3-9

4 **If you have no new mail, click the OK button.**

The dialog box disappears (Figure 3-10). You now are ready to send and receive mail. Notice the question mark adjacent to the mail icon disappears.

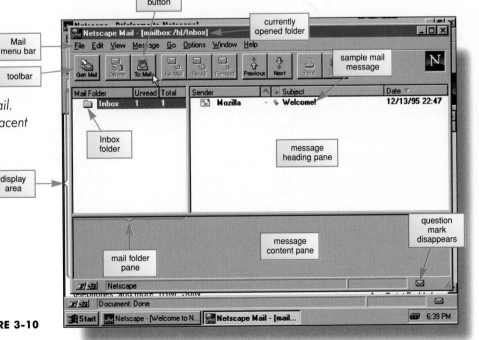

FIGURE 3-10

*Other***Ways**

1. Press ALT+W, press ALT+M

TABLE 3-1

BUTTON	FUNCTION
Get Mail	Connects to the mail server and brings any available mail messages into the Inbox.
Delete	Places the currently selected message in the message heading pane in the Trash folder.
To:Mail	Displays the Message Composition window for creating a new mail message. The To: field is empty.
Re:Mail	Displays the Message Composition window for replying to the current mail message. The To: field contains the e-mail address of the message's original sender.
Re:All	Displays the Message Composition window for replying to the current mail message. The To: field contains the e-mail address of all recipients of the message.
Forward	Displays the Message Composition window for forwarding the current mail message as an attachment. The To: field is empty. The original Subject: field is prefixed with Fwd.
Previous	Displays the previous unread message in the message heading pane.
Next	Displays the next unread message in the message heading pane.
Print	Prints the currently selected message in the message heading pane.
Stop	Halts any ongoing transmission of messages from the mail server.

The Netscape Mail window contains a menu bar, toolbar, and a display area. The toolbar buttons perform frequently used functions, such as composing a new message, checking to see if any new mail has arrived, and printing the current message. Table 3-1 contains the buttons and a brief explanation of their functions.

The display area is divided into three sections, or **panes**. The mail folder pane contains the names of **folders** where you can store mail messages. A folder is similar to a directory on a disk. Three folders usually are used with electronic mail. The **Inbox** folder contains unread mail messages just received from your Internet mail account. The **Outbox** folder contains mail messages you have composed, but not yet sent. The **Trash** folder contains mail messages you have deleted. This is a safety feature. You can retrieve messages you deleted if you later decide you want to keep them. Deleting mail messages from the Trash folder removes the messages permanently.

Because this is probably the first time you have used Netscape for electronic mail, only the Inbox has been created. The Outbox and Trash folders will be created automatically as you request activities that use them. You also can create your own folders. This allows you to organize your mail by sender, category, research topic, or any way you desire.

The second pane of the Mail window is the **message heading pane**, which contains summary information about the messages in the currently opened folder. Netscape opens the Inbox folder automatically when you first enter mail. The name of the currently opened folder is in the title bar (see Figure 3-10 on the previous page). The message heading pane contains one message, from Mozilla. This is a sample message from Netscape Communications Corporation that is generated automatically the very first time electronic mail is used. You might not see this message on your computer. Other messages may display in your mail box that were sent by the college or organization you attend or by one of your friends.

The third pane of the mail window is the **message content pane**, which contains the contents of the currently selected electronic mail message. If the mail message is larger than the display window, a scroll bar and scroll box will appear that allow you to display the entire message. You can now send mail using the Netscape Message Composition window.

More *About* **Creating Folders**

You can create a new mail folder by clicking File on the mail menu bar and then clicking New Folder.

Sending a Mail Message Using Netscape

When sending mail, you must provide the recipient's e-mail address, a brief one-line sentence, called the **subject**, that identifies the purpose or contents of the message, and the message itself.

The message then will be sent over the Internet. When it arrives at its destination, the destination computer stores the message in a special file using the receiver's account name as the filename. This file is the **mail box**. The messages will stay in the mail box until the receiver of the message starts a mail program, such as Netscape, and reads the incoming mail. The mail program will open the mail box and allow the individual to issue commands to read, save, delete, print, or otherwise manage electronic mail.

The following steps illustrate how to send a mail message to yourself. For you to successfully carry out these steps, you should substitute your electronic mail address wherever you see jordank@niia.net. The message then will be sent to your account. This is to ensure you will have a mail message to use while continuing through the section on e-mail in this project. If you do not have an electronic mail address, ask your instructor for information on how to obtain a mail account.

Steps **To Send a Mail Message**

1 **Click the To: Mail button on the toolbar (see Figure 3-10 on page NN 3.9).**

The Message Composition window displays (Figure 3-11). It contains a menu bar, a toolbar, and text boxes where you enter the electronic mail address of the recipient, the electronic mail addresses where any duplicate copies of the message are to be sent, the subject of the message, the names of any files you want to attach to the message, and the message itself. The insertion point is in the Mail To text box.

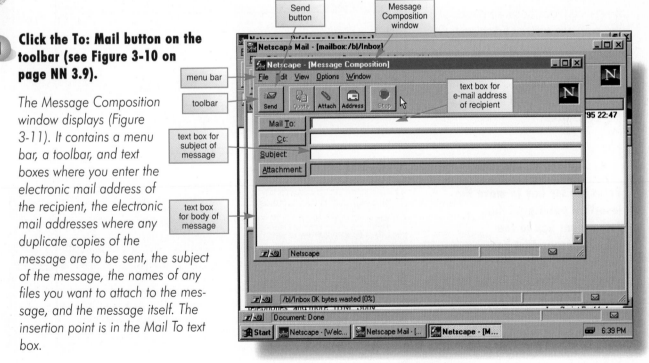

FIGURE 3-11

2 **With the insertion point in the Mail To text box, type your electronic mail address in the text box. Make sure you substitute your mail address for the address shown in the figure.**

The destination electronic mail address appears in the Mail To text box (Figure 3-12).

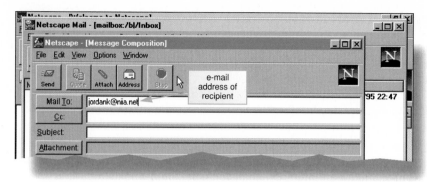

FIGURE 3-12

3 **Press the TAB key twice to move the insertion point past the Cc text box to the Subject text box and then type** Letterman's Top Ten **in the text box.**

The subject of the message displays in the Subject text box (Figure 3-13). The Cc text box is left blank because copies of the message are not being sent. Cc stands for Carbon copy. If you wanted to send a copy of a message to someone, you would enter the e-mail address of that person in the Cc text box.

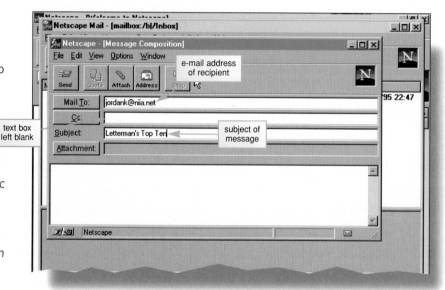

FIGURE 3-13

4 **Press the TAB key to move the insertion point past the Attachment box to the large message text box and then type** Did you see Letterman's Top Ten last night? You've GOT to see it. If you missed it, it's at http://www.cbs.com/ lateshow/ Check out number 4. Kurt **in the text box.**

The message displays in the message text box (Figure 3-14). The Attachment box is left blank because you do not want to include a disk file in this message. You can use the arrow keys to move around in the message to correct any errors you might have made.

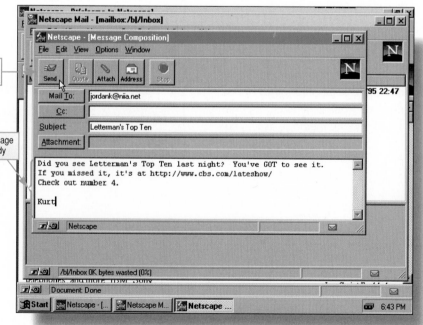

FIGURE 3-14

5 **Click the Send button on the toolbar.**

A message displays in the active link indicator of the Message Composition window indicating the mail server is being contacted (Figure 3-15). When the Message Composition window disappears, the message has been sent. The Netscape Mail window redisplays.

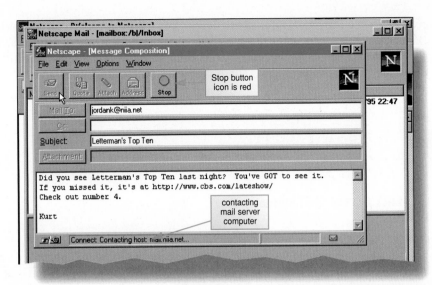

FIGURE 3-15

Other Ways

1. Press CTRL+M
2. Press ALT+F, press ALT+M

It is important to correctly indicate the content or purpose of the message in the subject line, not only when using electronic mail, but also in other Internet correspondence. This allows the recipient to categorize and screen mail without having to read each message. If your subject is vague, or missing, a recipient just may delete the message without reading it.

You can move around within the message using the arrow keys, making any desired corrections before clicking the Send button. If the message becomes so long it does not fit in the message text box you can scroll down, allowing more room for typing longer messages.

Adding Personality to Your Mail Messages

Even though the person reading your mail message might be on the other side of the world, you can still convey your personality and emotions along with the message. This is accomplished by including special combinations of characters, called **smiley faces**, or **smileys**, in your message. Table 3-2 contains several smiley faces and their meanings. The first smiley in Table 3-2 consists of three characters: a colon (:), a minus sign (-), and a right parenthesis ()). You might have to turn the page 90° clockwise to see the faces.

In addition to the smiley faces, several other character combinations, intended to save time and space, have become popular on the Internet. These combinations are abbreviations of frequently used phrases. Table 3-3 shows some of the more popular abbreviations.

Reading Electronic Mail Using Netscape

Notice in Figure 3-16, the Inbox contains only one mail message. This is the sample message that is generated automatically the first time you use Netscape mail. The message you sent to yourself is not yet contained in the Inbox, even though you sent the message using Netscape in previous steps. This mail is stored on a computer on the Internet called a **mail server**. A mail server maintains the mail boxes for many people.

TABLE 3-2	
SMILEY	*MEANING*
:-)	I'm happy/I'm smiling
:-(	I'm sad/I'm unhappy
;-)	Conveys sarcasm/knowing wink
O:-)	An angelic or innocent remark
:-D	I'm laughing
:-O	I'm surprised

TABLE 3-3	
ABBREVIATION	*MEANING*
ASAP	As soon as possible
BTW	By the way
CU	See you later
IMHO	In my humble opinion
NRN	No reply necessary
PLS	Please
THX	Thank you

The mail server will not allow you to read your mail until you have correctly identified yourself using your account name and password.

To check for newly arrived mail, you have to send a request to the mail server. The mail server then will deliver your mail to you, as shown in the following step.

Steps **To Contact the Mail Server**

1 **Click the Get Mail button on the toolbar.**

A message displays in the active link indicator indicating the progress of your request (Figure 3-16). When contacting the mail server computer this way, Netscape does not prompt you for your password again, because it remembers what you entered as the password in previous steps. All the mail messages the mail server has for you will be transferred to Netscape. When the messages arrive, summary information for each message appears in the message heading pane. The first part of the contents of the first message displays in the message display pane (Figure 3-17).

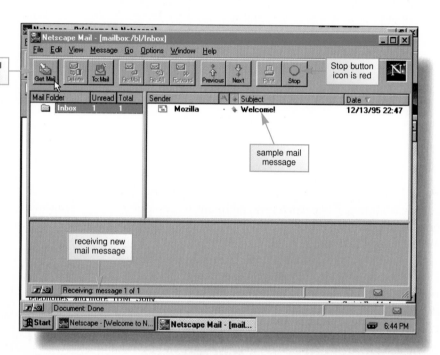

FIGURE 3-16

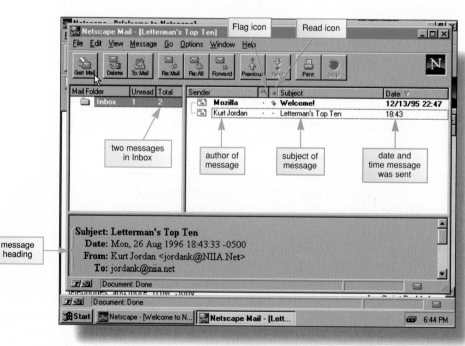

FIGURE 3-17

Other*Ways*

1. Press CTRL+T
2. Press ALT+F, press ALT+G

Each message heading contains the name of the author of the message, the contents of the subject line of the message, a Flag icon, a Read icon, and the date and time the message was sent. You can see how important the subject is when composing a message. Other people reading their mail will browse through the subjects, deciding which messages to read and which to disregard. If your subject is vague, or missing, chances are no one will read your message.

Other messages might display in the message heading pane. Some colleges and organizations send a welcome mail message to an account when it is first created. You might see this welcome message in the message heading list. One of your friends might have sent you a mail message already. Make note of the Letterman's Top Ten message and use it as you continue with the project.

Reading Mail Messages

You can now read the Letterman's Top Ten message in the Inbox, as shown in the following steps.

Steps To Read a Mail Message in Netscape

1

If the Letterman's Top Ten mail message is not in the message content pane, click the Letterman's Top Ten subject in the message heading pane.

The mail message appears in the message content pane (Figure 3-18). The message consists of a message heading and a message body. Only the message heading is visible in the message content pane.

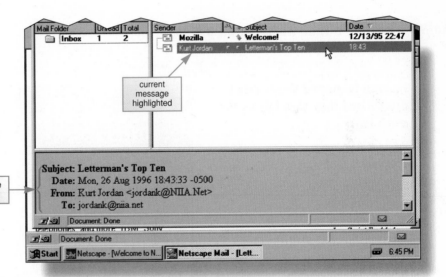

FIGURE 3-18

2

Use the scroll box to reveal more of the mail message.

The rest of the mail message displays (Figure 3-19). Notice the URL in the message is blue, indicating it can be used as an actual link to that Web page.

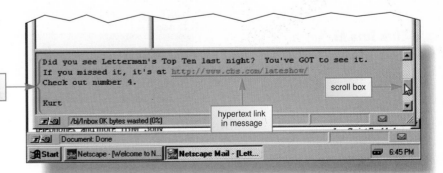

FIGURE 3-19

More *About*
Message Content Pane

You can resize the message content pane by dragging the separator bar up or down. This allows you to control how much of the message will display.

The message is made up of two parts. The first part consists of the **message heading**, containing the author of the message, the date and time the message was sent, the recipient of the message, and the subject line. The second part contains the **message** body. If the message is larger than the message field, you can scroll down the pane, revealing more of the message.

Notice the URL in the message is blue. This indicates that you can click the URL in the mail message and display that Web page. This is a powerful feature not found in other electronic mail programs.

You can display other mail messages by clicking the corresponding heading in the message heading pane. These messages will stay in your Inbox until you delete them.

Saving a Message on a Floppy Disk

Some messages you receive may be important enough that you will want to save them on a floppy disk. For example, a message may contain program source code or an answer to a problem that you will want for future reference. Perhaps you just want to preserve a record, or **audit trail**, of your correspondence. The following steps illustrate how to save the Letterman's Top Ten mail message on a floppy disk in drive B.

Steps To Save a Mail Message on a Floppy Disk

1 **Insert a formatted floppy disk in drive B and then click File on the menu bar.**

The File menu displays (Figure 3-20). It contains commands to perform functions such as create a new folder and remove messages from the Trash folder.

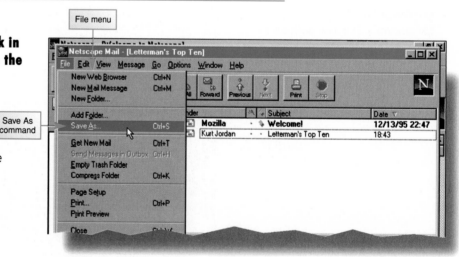

FIGURE 3-20

2 **Click Save As.**

The Save Messages As dialog box displays (Figure 3-21).

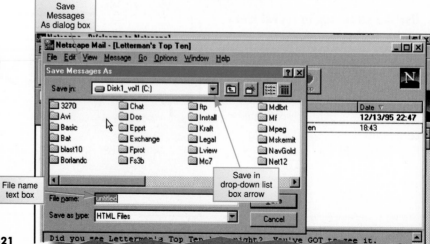

FIGURE 3-21

3 Type `topten.txt` **in the File name text box. Click the Save in box arrow to open the drop-down list box. Click 3½ Floppy [B:] to select drive B as the destination drive.**

The filename topten.txt replaces untitled (Figure 3-22). Drive B becomes the destination drive. The drive letter you choose may be different on your computer.

4 **Click the OK button to save the message.**

The Save Messages As dialog box disappears. The message has been saved to the floppy disk in drive B in a file called topten.txt.

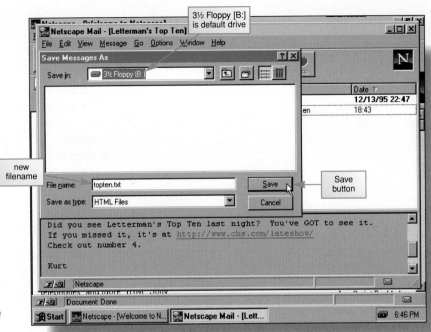

FIGURE 3-22

Recall that messages will stay in your Inbox until you delete them. The saving technique just illustrated is used to extract individual messages from your mail folders and store them separately in a file.

Printing a Mail Message

Netscape provides facilities for printing mail messages using the Print button on the toolbar. The following steps describe how to print a mail message.

 Steps To Print a Mail Message

1 **Ready the printer according to the printer instructions and then click the Print button on the toolbar.**

The Print dialog box displays (Figure 3-23). This is the same Print dialog box shown in the section on printing in Project 1 on NN 1.41.

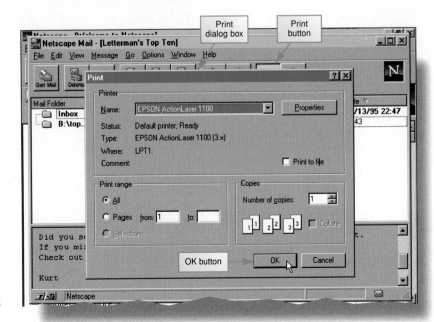

FIGURE 3-23

2 **Click the OK button.**

The Printing Progress dialog box will display. When printing is complete, retrieve the printout (Figure 3-24).

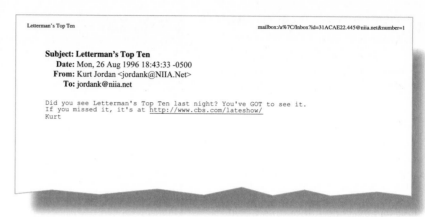

Letterman's Top Ten
mailbox:/a%7C/Inbox?id=31ACAE22.445@niia.net&number=1

Subject: Letterman's Top Ten
Date: Mon, 26 Aug 1996 18:43:33 -0500
From: Kurt Jordan <jordank@NIIA.Net>
To: jordank@niia.net

Did you see Letterman's Top Ten last night? You've GOT to see it.
If you missed it, it's at http://www.cbs.com/lateshow/
Kurt

FIGURE 3-24

OtherWays

1. Press CTRL+P
2. Press ALT+F, press ALT+P

The printed message contains both the message heading and message body.

Deleting a Mail Message

Once you have read, and possibly saved your e-mail, you should remove unwanted mail messages from the Inbox. If you do not delete mail messages, the list of messages will get very long. In addition, allowing old messages to accumulate in your mail box wastes disk space. The following steps delete the Letterman's Top Ten mail message.

Steps **To Delete a Mail Message**

1 **Click the Letterman's Top Ten message heading.**

The message is highlighted (Figure 3-25).

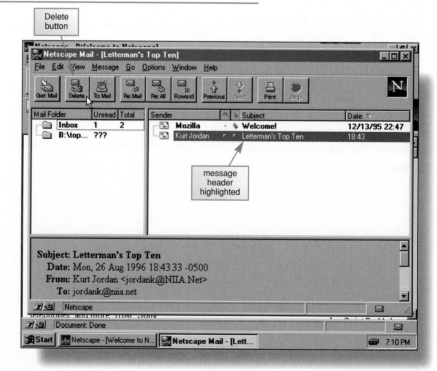

FIGURE 3-25

2 Click the Delete button on the toolbar.

The Letterman's Top Ten message disappears from the message heading pane (Figure 3-26). The Welcome! message becomes highlighted and that message's contents display in the message content pane. The Letterman's Top Ten message has been removed from the Inbox and placed in the Trash folder.

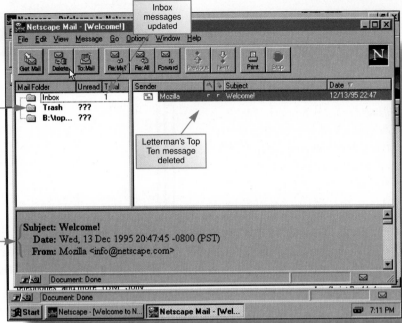

FIGURE 3-26

▶ *Other***Ways**

1. Press DELETE
2. Press ALT+E, press ALT+O
3. Click File, click Empty Trash Folder

Notice the Trash folder was created automatically when you deleted the Letterman's Top Ten message. As you delete messages from the Inbox, the Trash folder will grow, increasing with the addition of the deleted messages. You should open the Trash folder regularly and remove the deleted messages by highlighting them and clicking the Delete button, as shown in the previous steps. You can open the Trash folder by clicking it.

Using an Address Book

With the World Wide Web crossing international borders, your list of electronic mail contacts is likely to be large. Keeping track of all those electronic mail addresses is easy using an electronic address book. Like a bookmark list, the **address book** is a file containing the names and electronic mail addresses of those persons with whom you frequently correspond. The following steps show how to display Netscape's address book.

◆ **More** *About*
Trash Folder

You can empty the entire trash folder by clicking File on the mail menu bar and then clicking Empty Trash Folder.

 Steps To Display the Address Book

1 Click Window on the menu bar.

The Window menu displays (Figure 3-27). The Address Book command displays the Address Book window.

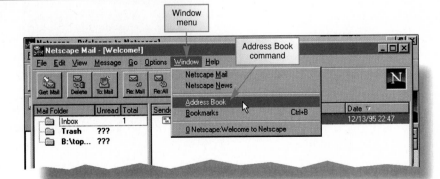

FIGURE 3-27

2 Click Address Book.

The Address Book window displays (Figure 3-28). Figure 3-28 shows no addresses listed, however, addresses may be listed on your computer. The Address Book window includes a menu bar containing menus with commands used to manage address books and their entries.

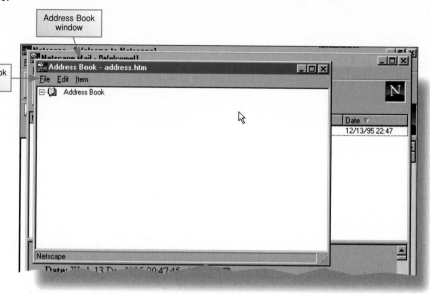

FIGURE 3-28

OtherWays

1. Press ALT +W, press ALT+A

The Address Book window is similar to the Bookmarks window shown in Project 1. Addresses are listed in the window in a hierarchical format. New addresses are added to the end of the list. Features for organizing addresses exist within the Edit and Item menus. You can add new addresses to the Address Book, as shown in the following steps.

 Steps To Add an Address to the Address Book

1 Click Item on the menu bar.

The Item menu displays (Figure 3-29). The commands allow you to add a new address or a new list category and organize your address book entries into groups.

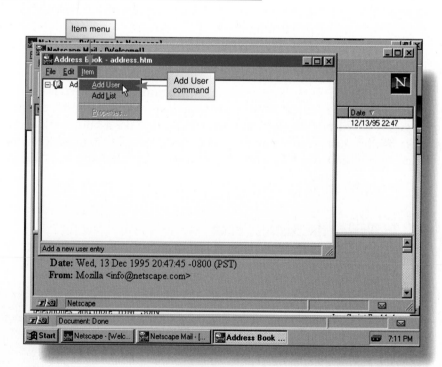

FIGURE 3-29

2 **Click Add User.**

The Address Book dialog box opens and the Properties sheet displays (Figure 3-30). The sheet contains text boxes for entering a nickname, the full name of a person, the e-mail address, and a brief description of the address book entry. The **nickname** can be the name of a person, a place, a company, or any word or phrase that you can remember easily. The nickname is the name you will place in the Mail To: text box when composing a new message. The insertion point is in the Nick Name text box.

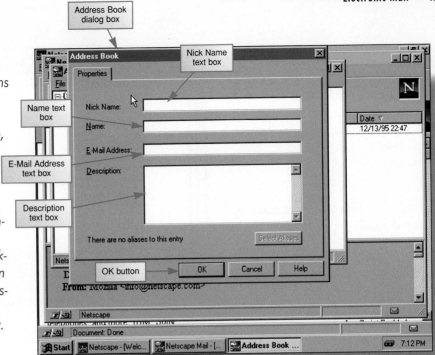

FIGURE 3-30

3 **Type** kj **in the Nick Name text box.**

The nickname kj displays in the text box (Figure 3-31).

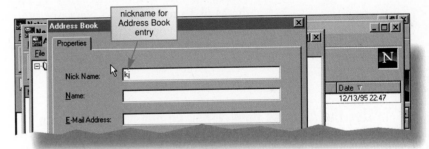

FIGURE 3-31

4 **Press the TAB key to move the insertion point to the Name text box. Type** Kurt Jordan **in the Name text box. Press the TAB key to move the insertion point to the E-Mail Address text box. Type** jordank@niia.net **in the E-Mail Address text box.**

The name and e-mail address of the Address Book entry display (Figure 3-32).

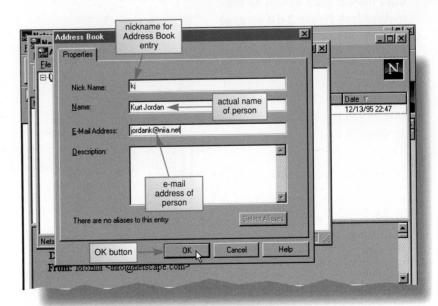

FIGURE 3-32

5 **Click the OK button to save the Address Book entry.**

The Address Book dialog box disappears, revealing the Address Book window (Figure 3-33). Notice an entry for Kurt Jordan is last on the list.

6 **Click the Close button to close the window.**

The Address Book window disappears, revealing the Netscape Mail window.

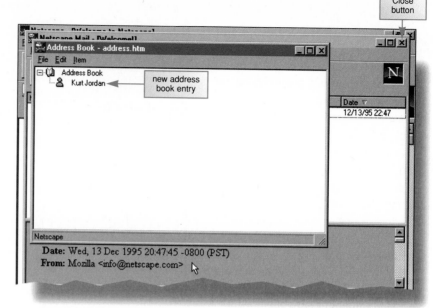

FIGURE 3-33

*Other***Ways**

1. Press ALT+I, press ALT+A

To use one of the entries in your Address Book, you supply the nickname in the Mail To text box and Netscape will substitute automatically the electronic mail address you specified in the Address Book entry. The following steps show how to retrieve an electronic mail address from the Address Book using the nickname.

Steps **To Use the Address Book When Composing a Message**

1 **Click the To: Mail button on the toolbar (see Figure 3-10 on page NN 3.9). Type kj in the Mail To text box.**

The Message Composition window displays (Figure 3-34). The nickname kj displays in the Mail To text box.

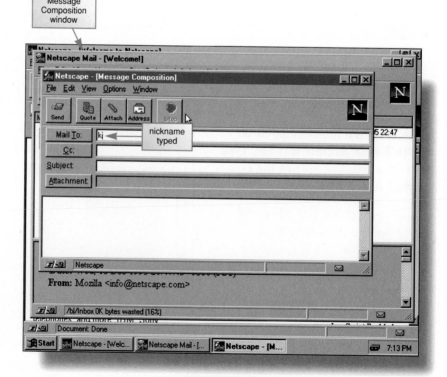

FIGURE 3-34

2 Press the TAB key to move the insertion point to the next text box.

The nickname is replaced automatically with the name and electronic mail address of the corresponding Address Book entry (Figure 3-35). You can compose the message and send it using the Send button on the toolbar.

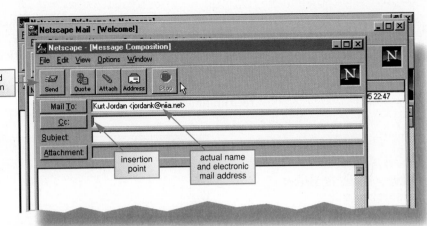

FIGURE 3-35

You can see how setting up nicknames for those persons with whom you frequently correspond can save time and prevent you from having to remember long, sometimes cryptic electronic mail addresses.

Exiting Electronic Mail

You have successfully sent, received, and managed mail messages and created entries in an electronic Address Book. After managing your mail, you can exit the Mail window, as shown in the following step.

TO EXIT ELECTRONIC MAIL

Step 1: If necessary, click the Close button to close the Message Composition window.
Step 2: Click the Close button to close the Mail window.

The Mail window disappears. The Netscape home page displays.

It is important that, if you receive your electronic mail, you remember to exit completely from the Netscape program when you are finished using Netscape. Recall that Netscape remembers your password after you enter it to receive mail. If you do not exit Netscape completely, the next person to use that computer can receive any new mail that may have arrived for you since you last read your mail. Exiting completely will cause Netscape to forget the password and protect your mail from unauthorized access. Exiting Netscape is described at the end of this project.

Newsgroups

It is human nature for people with similar interests to be drawn together to discuss and share their thoughts, information, opinions, and research. Sometimes, people form clubs or discussion groups where they can talk and exchange ideas about their mutual interests.

A very large number of electronic discussion groups called **newsgroups** are available on the Internet. Using Netscape, you can **post**, or send, to the newsgroup your thoughts and opinions about a particular topic and read what other people have to say. The articles that accumulate on a particular topic are called a **thread**. Figure 3-36 shows some articles and threads from a newsgroup called rec.running.

More *About* **Newsgroup Articles**

You can find pictures, movies, and sound clips available in newsgroups. Look for the words, pictures, movies, or audio, in the newsgroup name.

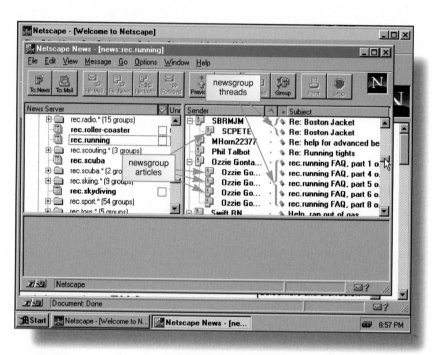

FIGURE 3-36

TABLE 3-4	
PREFIX	*DESCRIPTION*
alt	Groups on alternative topics
biz	Business topics
comp	Computer topics
gnu	GNU Software Foundation topics
ieee	Electrical engineering topics
info	Information about various topics
misc	Miscellaneous topics
news	Groups pertaining to Usenet newsgroups
rec	Recreational topics
sci	Science topics
talk	Various conversation groups

Newsgroups exist on vendor products such as Novell, Microsoft, IBM, and UNIX, on subjects such as recipes, gardening, and music, or on just about any other topic you can think of. The discussion topics are organized into broad categories, some of which are listed in Table 3-4.

A newsgroup name might begin with one of these prefixes, followed by one or more words that narrow down the main topic of the group. The newsgroup name comp.lang.pascal is a group interested in computers. The group further limits discussions to programming languages, specifically, Pascal. The rec.running newsgroup (Figure 3-36) is a recreational newsgroup with discussions concerning topics related to the sport of running.

These newsgroup prefixes are not the only ones used. New newsgroups are being created everyday. Some colleges and universities have their own newsgroups on topics such as administrative information, tutoring, and campus organizations.

Accessing Usenet with Netscape

Usenet is the term used to describe the collection of computer sites that has agreed to share and forward the thousands of discussion groups. The following steps illustrate how you can use Netscape to access Usenet newsgroups.

Steps **To Access Newsgroups in Netscape**

1 **Click Window on the menu bar.**

The Window menu displays (Figure 3-37). The Netscape News command is used to access newsgroups.

FIGURE 3-37

2 **Click Netscape News.**

The Netscape News window displays (Figure 3-38). The window consists of a menu bar, toolbar, and three panes to display newsgroup and article information.

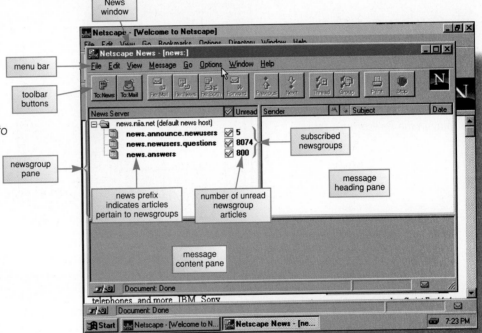

FIGURE 3-38

*Other***Ways**

1. Press ALT+W, press ALT+N

Like the Mail window, the Netscape News window is divided into three parts, or panes. The **newsgroup pane** contains the names of newsgroups, subscribed check boxes, and the number of unread messages. The **message heading pane** contains the list of available articles from a chosen newsgroup. Each line in the pane represents one article and contains the name of the sender of the article, a Flag icon, a Read icon, the contents of the subject of the article, and the date and time the article was sent. The **message content pane** displays the contents of an article.

When first accessing newsgroups, the newsgroup pane contains the list of newsgroups to which a user currently is subscribed. **Subscribed** means you have selected these groups as the ones you want to visit most frequently. The newsgroups you see listed are the default newsgroups to which everyone is automatically subscribed when first accessing Usenet. The default newsgroups may be different at your school or organization.

More *About*
Newsgroups

Most Internet service providers make available newsgroup access as part of their Internet services.

Netscape will keep the names of subscribed newsgroups in a special file and make them available every time you click Netscape News. You will subscribe to newsgroups later in the project.

Notice the prefix of the listed newsgroup names is news. This indicates the topic of these groups is Usenet and newsgroups. These are only a few of the thousands of newsgroups available. The following steps show how to display a list of all the available newsgroups.

Steps **To Display All Available Newsgroups**

---

① **Click Options on the Netscape News menu bar.**

The Options menu displays (Figure 3-39). The Options menu contains several commands to manage newsgroups. The Show All Newsgroups command causes a list of all available newsgroup names to display in the newsgroups pane.

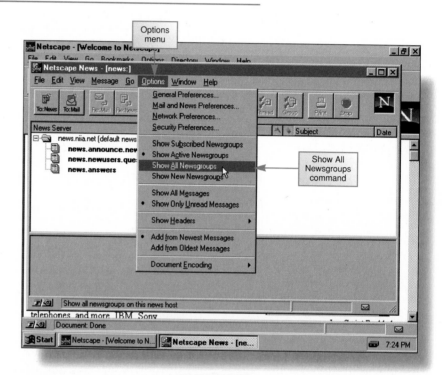

FIGURE 3-39

② **Click Show All Newsgroups.**

A message displays in the active link indicator of the News window indicating the status of the transfer (Figure 3.40). Remember, thousands of newsgroups exixt. The transfer may take a few moments.

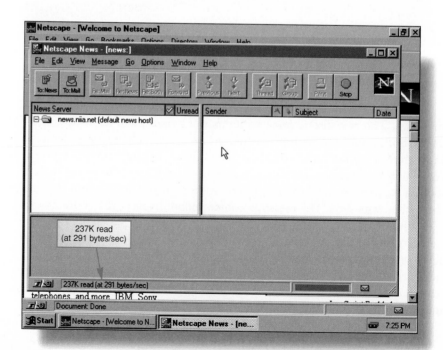

FIGURE 3-40

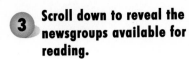

3 **Scroll down to reveal the newsgroups available for reading.**

The list of newsgroups displays in the newsgroup pane (Figure 3-41). The list contains individual newsgroups and collections of newsgroups that all start with a common prefix.

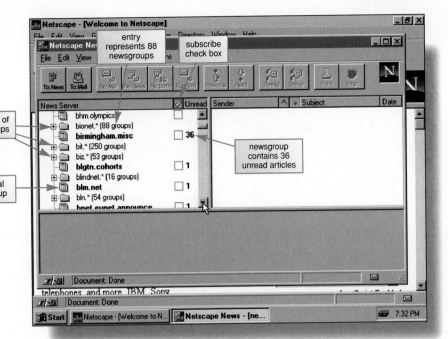

FIGURE 3-41

The list contains two types of entries. The first, identified by the pages icon, are newsgroups you can enter to read articles. These entries also have the number of unread articles in the newsgroup and a check box that can be clicked to subscribe to the newsgroup. The second type of entry, identified by the folder icon, represents a collection of newsgroups that all begin with the letters you see preceding the asterisk (*). The number on each line represents the number of newsgroups that start with that prefix. Clicking one of these lines displays a hierarchical list below that line with links to newsgroups that all start with that specific prefix. This makes the list of all newsgroups somewhat shorter and easier to scan.

The toolbar buttons allow you to post a new article to the newsgroup, send mail to an article author, and manage articles in the newsgroup. You will use the buttons to send your own newsgroup article later in the project.

Selecting a Newsgroup

With the list of available newsgroups displayed, you can select one and read the articles. To illustrate how to select a newsgroup, the following steps show how to display the rec.animals.wildlife newsgroup and then find articles about skunks. Recall that newsgroups that begin with rec are recreation related. See Table 3-4 on page NN 3.24.

◆ **More** *About* **Newsgroup Window Pane**

The column widths and pane sizes can be adjusted in the newsgroup window in a manner similar to the electronic mail columns and panes.

Steps To Display the rec.animals.wildlife Newsgroup

1 Scroll down the newsgroup pane until the rec.* folder appears.

The rec.* folder represent newsgroups that start with rec (Figure 3-42). Notice that 596 recreational newsgroups are available.

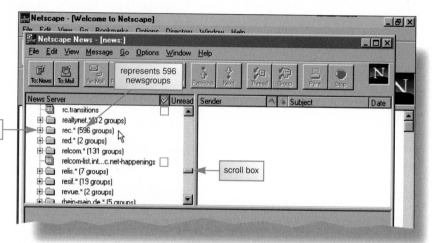

FIGURE 3-42

2 Double-click the rec.* line.

The list of rec newsgroups displays below the rec.* folder (Figure 3-43). The groups are in alphabetical order. Several entries represent further subdivisions of rec newsgroups. The rec. animals.wildlife newsgroup is first on the list of rec newsgroups.

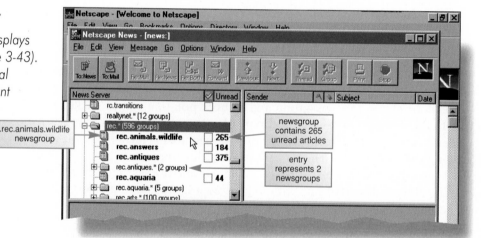

FIGURE 3-43

3 Click rec.animals.wildlife.

The list of available rec.animals.wildlife articles displays in the message heading pane (Figure 3-44). The list represents available articles to be read. The format of each line is similar to an electronic mail message heading line, with the name of the author, a Flag icon, a Read icon, the subject of the article, and the date and time the article was sent.

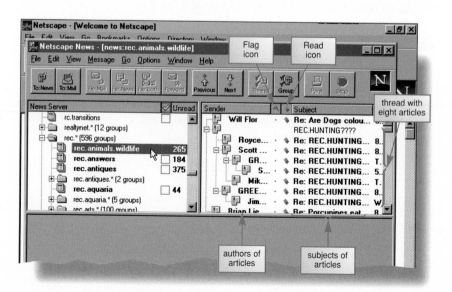

FIGURE 3-44

The article icons at the right side of the message heading pane represent the logical connection between the articles. You can see one eight-article thread.

Reading Newsgroup Articles

Each entry in the message heading pane in Figure 3-44 reflects the contents of the subject line that appears inside the article. This allows you to look at the subjects of the articles to decide whether to read them without actually having to display the article. You now can read an article, as shown in the following steps.

Steps **To Read a Newsgroup Article**

1 **Scroll through the message heading pane using the scroll box. Click the skunk defumigation entry. This is the first of two skunk articles.**

The news article displays in the message content pane (Figure 3-45). The format is similar to an electronic mail message, with an article heading and body. The number of unread articles in the newsgroup is updated. The Read icon for the article is turned off.

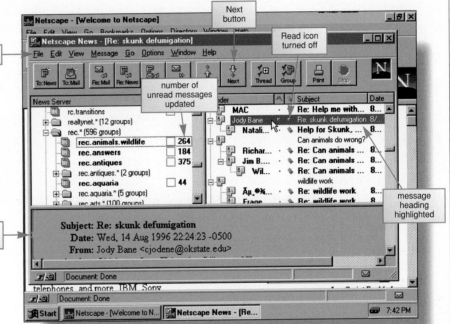

FIGURE 3-45

2 **Scroll down to reveal the body of the article.**

The body of the article displays (Figure 3-46).

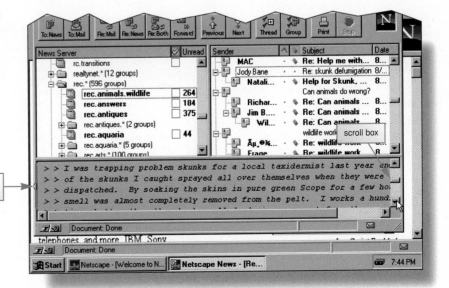

FIGURE 3-46

TABLE 3-5

BUTTON	FUNCTION
To:News	Displays the Message Composition window for creating a new news message.
To:Mail	Displays the Message Composition window for creating a new mail message.
Re:Mail	Displays the Message Composition window for replying to the current message's sender. The To field is pre-addressed.
Re:News	Displays the Message Composition window for replying to the current news message thread.
Re:Both	Displays the Message Composition window for replying to the current news message thread and replying by mail to the message's sender.
Forward	Displays the Message Composition window for forwarding the current news message as an attachment. The To field is blank. The original Subject field is prefixed with Fwd.
Previous	Displays the previous unread message in the thread.
Next	Displays the next unread message in the thread.
Thread	Marks messages in the thread as read.
Group	Marks all messages in the group as read.
Print	Prints the currently selected message in the message heading field.
Stop	Halts any ongoing transmission of messages from the news server.

The article heading contains the subject of the article, the date and time the article was posted, the person who posted the article, and the organization from which the article was sent. Following the heading is the body, which contains the contents of the article.

Notice in Figure 3-46 on the previous page the toolbar at the top of the window. Table 3-5 summarizes the functions of the buttons.

After reading this article, you can move to the next article in the newsgroup by clicking the Next button on the toolbar, as shown in the following steps.

Steps To Read the Next Newsgroup Article

1 **Click the Next button on the toolbar.**

The next article in the newsgroup displays in the display area (Figure 3-47). The number of unread articles in the newsgroup is updated. The Read icon for the article is turned off.

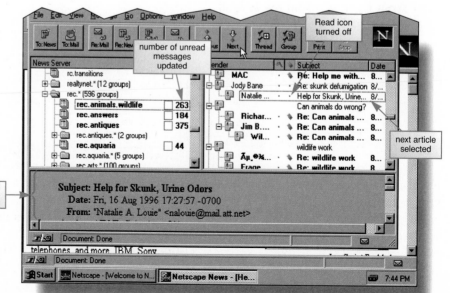

FIGURE 3-47

2 **Scroll down to reveal the body of the article.**

The body of the next article in the thread displays (Figure 3-48). The article contains comments on a product for countering the smell of a skunk.

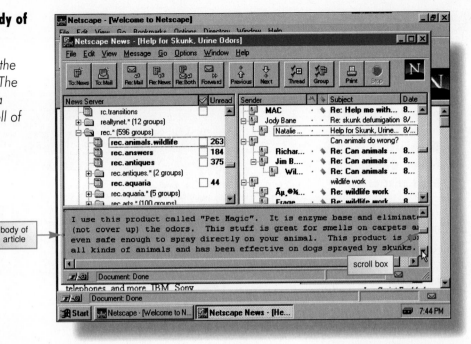

body of article

FIGURE 3-48

You can continue to follow the line of discussion in this thread by clicking the Next button or clicking one of the other article headings to move to another thread.

Saving and Printing Newsgroup Articles

You almost certainly will want to save news articles that contain interesting or important information on disk. Saving articles is accomplished the same way as saving electronic mail messages. Printing articles also is accomplished the same way as printing electronic mail messages. See page NN 3.16 for saving and page NN 3.17 for printing.

Selecting Another Newsgroup

When you are finished reading the articles, you must leave this newsgroup and select another before you can read those articles. To access another newsgroup, just double-click the newsgroup name in the newsgroup pane and follow the previous instructions to read the articles. You now have learned how to display, save, and print individual newsgroup articles and move to another newsgroup. The next section shows you how to post newsgroup articles.

Posting Newsgroup Articles

Newsgroups contain a treasure chest of information and amusement. It is likely a time may come when you will want to post, or send, an article to a newsgroup. The following steps show how to submit a newsgroup article by posting to the news.misc group. This is a newsgroup just for miscellaneous purposes. This way, you will not disturb any other newsgroup participants with your practice articles. When you are familiar with the posting process, you can select an appropriate newsgroup to send your thoughts and opinions.

Other**Ways**

1. Press ALT+G, press ALT+N

More *About* **Next and Previous Buttons**

The Next and Previous buttons move through the articles in a thread similar to the way the Back and Forward buttons move through the pages in Netscape's history list.

Steps To Post a Newsgroup Article

1 Scroll through the list of newsgroups in the newsgroup pane until the news.* folder displays. Double-click the news.* folder. Double-click the news.misc entry.

The articles in the news. misc newsgroup display (Figure 3-49). Notice that some test articles are contained in this newsgroup.

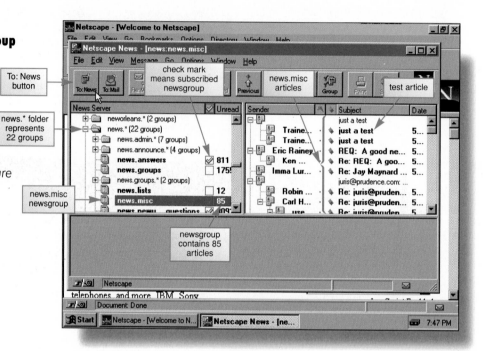

FIGURE 3-49

2 Click the To: News button on the article toolbar.

The Netscape Message Composition window displays (Figure 3-50). Notice this window is similar to the mail Message Composition window, with text fields where information for the article heading and the article body are typed. The Newsgroups text box contains the name of the newsgroup.

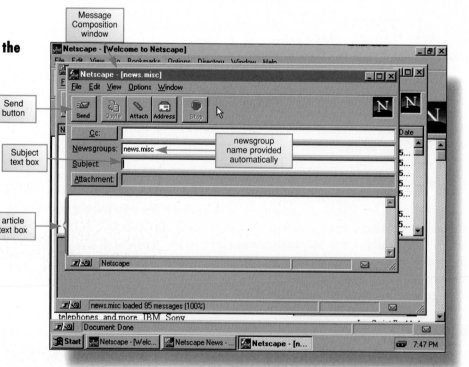

FIGURE 3-50

③ Type test message **in the Subject text box. Press the TAB key to move the insertion point to the message text box. Type** Newsgroups offer discussion on many diverse topics.

The subject indicates correctly this is a test message and can be safely disregarded by anyone browsing through the newsgroup (Figure 3-51). Recall that subjects are important parts of Internet communications.

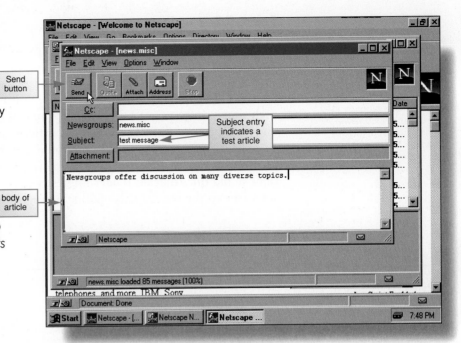

FIGURE 3-51

④ Click the Send button.

The Netscape news.misc window redisplays. Other people with newsgroup access now can read your article. You can check to see if your article is available by requesting the articles in the newsgroup again by double-clicking the newsgroup name in the newsgroup pane.

⑤ Double-click news.misc newsgroup in the newsgroup pane to request re-loading of the articles from the news server. Scroll down in the message heading pane to see your article.

The articles are re-loaded from the newsgroup server computer (Figure 3-52). Notice that 86 articles now are available. Your article should be toward the end of the list.

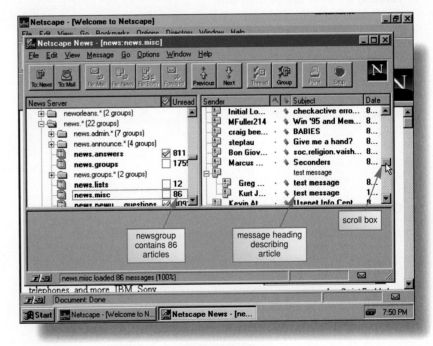

FIGURE 3-52

You learned how to post an article to a newsgroup. You now can return to the list of newsgroups and select another to read or to which you can post articles.

Subscribing to Newsgroups

Remember that the list of newsgroups is very large, with thousands of newsgroups. Having to retrieve and then scroll through the list whenever you want to access your favorite newsgroups can get tiresome and wastes time. You can instruct Netscape to store a list of your favorite newsgroups and present them each time you go to read news. Then you can choose from among this shorter list, and then proceed directly to read the articles that interest you.

The list of newsgroups is stored on a disk file. The process of building this list is called **subscribing**. You can include new, interesting newsgroups you find and remove old ones that no longer interest you. The following steps illustrate how to subscribe to the rec.animals.wildlife newsgroup.

Steps **To Subscribe to a Newsgroup**

1 **Scroll through the newsgroup pane until the rec.animals.wildlife newsgroup displays. In the subscribe column, which is the column with the Subscribe icon, click the check box.**

A check mark appears in the check box indicating you have subscribed to the newsgroup (Figure 3-53).

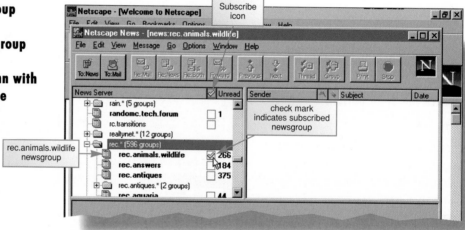

FIGURE 3-53

2 **Click Options on the menu bar.**

The Options menu displays (Figure 3-54). Clicking Show Subscribed Newsgroups will display the list of newsgroups to which you have subscribed.

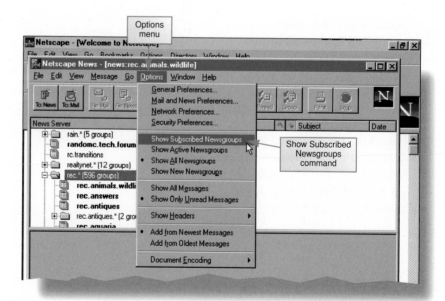

FIGURE 3-54

② Click Show Subscribed Newsgroups.

The list of subscribed newsgroups displays in the newsgroup pane, with the newly subscribed newsgroup added to the list (Figure 3-55). Notice the rec.animals.wildlife entry displays at the bottom of the list. It currently contains 266 unread articles, which is three more than when you displayed the articles earlier.

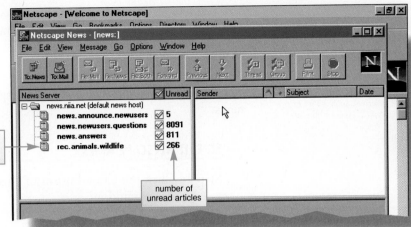

FIGURE 3-55

OtherWays

1. Press ALT+F, press ALT+D

Now when you access newsgroups from within Netscape, this list will display after you click Netscape News on the Window menu, and you can proceed directly to your favorite newsgroups without having to retrieve the long list of newsgroups.

Unsubscribing from a Newsgroup

When you no longer want a particular newsgroup to appear in your list of subscribed newsgroups, you can remove the newsgroup from the list. This process is called **unsubscribing.** The following step shows how to unsubscribe from the rec.animals.wildlife newsgroup.

 Steps To Unsubscribe from a Newsgroup

① Click the check box on the rec.animals.wildlife newsgroup entry.

The check mark disappears (Figure 3-56), indicating you wish to unsubscribe from this newsgroup. When you return to newsgroups later, the rec.animals.wildlife group will not display.

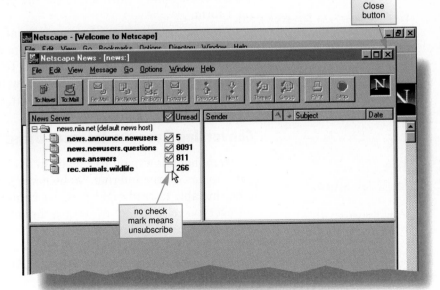

FIGURE 3-56

More *About*
New Newsgroups

Newsgroups are being used as a tool in courses being taught over the Internet. Instructors can post a question and all the students can respond and follow the thread.

You have learned how to display lists of newsgroups, read and post articles, and subscribe to and unsubscribe from newsgroups.

Exiting Netscape News

When you are finished reading newsgroup articles, you can exit Netscape news.

TO EXIT NETSCAPE NEWS

Step 1: Click the Close button to close the News window.

Netscape's home page redisplays.

Articles posted to newsgroups can be read by anyone who has access to the newsgroups and has Netscape or some other news reader program.

When using newsgroups or electronic mail to converse with people on the Internet, a time lag occurs between when a message is sent and when the message is read. Mail and newsgroup articles accumulate over time, waiting for you to run the appropriate program to read them. If live, real-time conversation is more to your liking, this communication method is available on the World Wide Web using a service called WebChat.

 ebChat

Netscape does more than just display Web pages. On certain types of pages, you can add your comments and then send them over the Internet. These special pages can contain **forms** in which you type information, such as a name and address. The form usually contains a button you click to send the information back to the Web site from which the page originated. Check boxes, option buttons, menus, selection lists, and a button to clear the information you enter all may be included on a form.

You can use the forms for entering information to query databases, order merchandise, send electronic mail, post newsgroup articles, fill out surveys, and communicate with other Internet users. To demonstrate how to use Netscape forms, the following steps show you how to engage in live conversations using a World Wide Web service called WebChat.

Conversing Over the Internet Using WebChat

WebChat allows you to engage in live, ongoing conversations with other participants on the Internet. WebChat is similar to a computerized party line, with everyone able to read other people's comments and type his or her own comments for everyone else to see. All this occurs in the time it takes to redisplay a Web page. WebChat can have hundreds of people all trying to converse at the same time. The WebChat page will contain a number of the most recent comments from the active WebChat participants. As new comments appear, old ones are removed.

More *About*
WebChat Sites

Some WebChat servers allow you to create private chat rooms that are protected by a password. Only those who know the password can participate in the conversation.

Connecting to a WebChat Session

The following steps show how to connect to the WebChat service at the Baltic Internet Plaza in Sweden. Because WebChat uses Web pages for communication, you are required to supply the URL of the WebChat Web site. Be sure to replace the name kurt with your own name when following these steps.

Steps To Connect to a WebChat Session

1 **Click in the location text box to highlight the current URL. Type** http://bip.concept.se/ index4.htm **in the location text box. Press the ENTER key.**

The BiP - Baltic Internet Plaza - BiP Web page displays (Figure 3-57). This page contains a link to a Web page where you can enter information necessary to use WebChat.

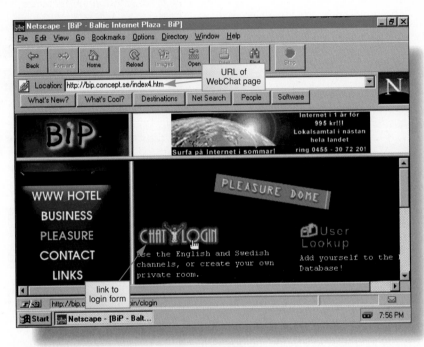

FIGURE 3-57

2 **Click the CHAT LOGIN link.**

The WebChat login form displays (Figure 3-58). The form contains a text box for your name, a drop-down list box listing different conversations and further down the page, a button to display the WebChat page.

FIGURE 3-58

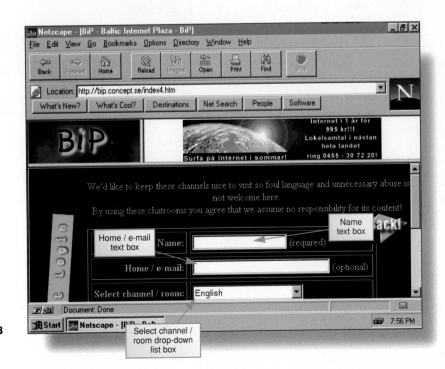

3 **Click the Name text box and then type your name in the text box. Click the Home/e-mail text box and type your electronic mail address.**

The name and electronic mail address used to identify your comments display in the text boxes (Figure 3-59). The name does not have to be your real name. It could be a nickname, or something that reflects your personality.

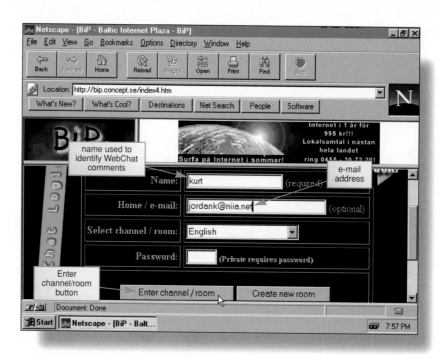

FIGURE 3-59

4 **Scroll down to reveal the Enter channel/room button. Click the Enter channel/room button.**

The Webchat - English Web page displays (Figure 3-60). There are comments from two WebChat participants: Falthar and Monica. The Internet address and the day and time the comment was sent appear after the name of the participant.

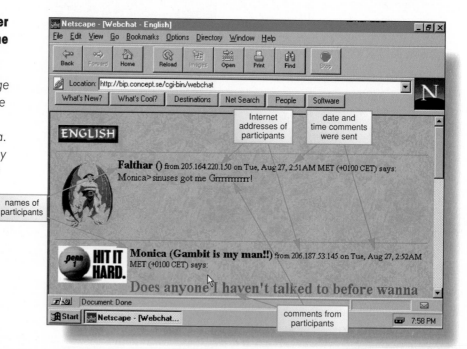

FIGURE 3-60

5 Scroll down to reveal the WebChat form.

The WebChat form displays (Figure 3-61). This form includes a Chat/Update button used to request a fresh page of comments, a large text box where your comments are typed, and option buttons to control font size, formatting, and color. Notice the comment indicating you have joined the WebChat conversation.

comment indicating participation in WebChat

Chat/Update button

comment text box

font and color option buttons

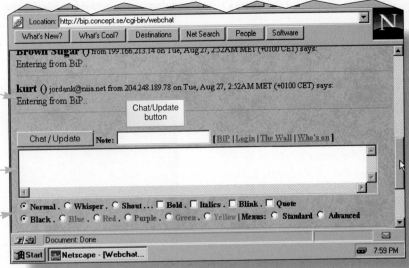

FIGURE 3-61

The chat page is made up of two parts. The first part contains the comments from the chat participants in the order they arrived, with the older comments at the top and the newer comments toward the bottom of the page. Each comment is made up of a name, the date and time, and the actual text of the comment. In Figure 3-60, the names Falthar and Monica are shown.

The second part of the page contains the form where you will enter your comments and request that the page be updated with fresh comments. You must redisplay the WebChat page to see fresh comments because the page is actually a snapshot of the comments that existed at the time you requested the page by clicking the Enter channel/room button, as shown in Figure 3-59 on page NN 3.38. As comments are sent by participants, they are added to the bottom of the page.

More *About*
Updating Comments

Some chat services allow you to customize the session so it automatically will display new comments every few minutes.

Participating in WebChat Conversations

After logging in, you can join in the conversations on the chat page as shown in the following steps.

 Steps To Converse on WebChat

1 With the bottom of the WebChat page displayed, click the comment text box.

An insertion point displays in the top left corner of the comment text box.

Chat/Update button

2 Type a message that identifies who you are and where you are located, such as the message shown in Figure 3-62.

comment to send to WebChat

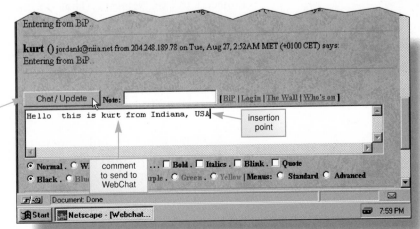

FIGURE 3-62

3 **Click the Chat/Update button.**

The chat page redisplays with your comment inserted on the page (Figure 3-63). Participants now can see your comment. Other people's comments will be placed below yours. Recall, you have to reload the page to see the new comments by clicking the Chat/Update button.

comment displayed on chat page

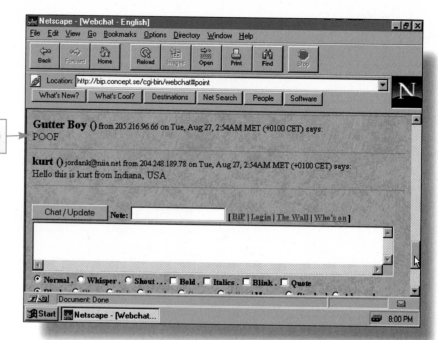

4 **Click the Chat/Update button.**

The chat page redisplays. New comments will be added after the comment you entered in Step 2. You can continue the conversation in this manner, reading what other people have to say, and entering your own comments.

FIGURE 3-63

Using the techniques and steps just presented, you have participated successfully in a WebChat conversation. If you have trouble following the dialog, do not be discouraged. Hundreds of people may be trying to talk all at the same time. WebChat displays the lines people type in the order they are received, making it difficult to follow what one person types because the comments are interspersed with comments from other people who are trying to have their own conversations.

As you continue to participate in WebChat, you will get better at deciphering this non-sequential method of conversation. Be aware. WebChat is totally unregulated. People can say whatever they please, including things that may be offensive.

Exiting Netscape

When you are finished chatting with WebChat, follow the steps discussed in Project 1 to exit Netscape. That step is summarized below.

TO EXIT NETSCAPE

Step 1: Click the Close button.

The Windows 95 desktop displays.

WebChat is not the only way to carry on live conversations over the Internet. Another method of conversation, using one of the traditional Internet services, is available with a program called Netscape Chat, or NetChat.

NetChat

Chatting over the Internet was available long before the World Wide Web appeared. Live conversation capabilities were available using an Internet service called **Internet Relay Chat,** or **IRC**. To use IRC, you connected to a special computer configured as the chat server, supplied your name, and joined one of the ongoing conversations. Like most of the other traditional Internet service programs, IRC is command-line oriented. You had to learn several commands in order to successfully use IRC.

Fortunately, a program now exists that serves as an easy method of participating in IRC discussions, just as Netscape serves as an easy method to access the resources on the World Wide Web. This program is **Netscape Chat,** or **NetChat,** and is available on many computers on the Internet, including Netscape Communications Corporation's FTP site. Project 2 demonstrates how to obtain a copy of NetChat.

To demonstrate using NetChat, you will connect to an IRC computer and converse with other IRC users there. When you carry out the following steps, be sure to substitute your own name wherever you see Kurt Jordan and your own nickname wherever you see kurtj. This will ensure your comments will not be confused with someone else's comments.

More *About* **Chat Programs**

There are other programs that can be used to participate in IRC conversations. One such program on UNIX systems is called irc.

 Steps To Start the NetChat Program

1 **If you are still in Netscape, exit the program by clicking the Close button, and then click the Start button on the taskbar. Point to Programs. Point to Netscape Chat 32bit. Point to Netscape Chat 32bit.**

The Windows 95 desktop displays as shown in Figure 3-64.

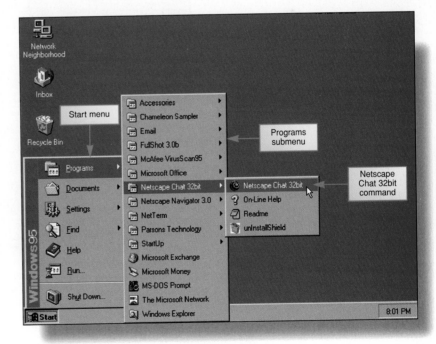

FIGURE 3-64

2 **Click Netscape Chat 32bit.**

The Console - Netscape Chat window displays (Figure 3-65). The Server Connection dialog box displays. The dialog box consists of two areas. The upper area contains information about the IRC server to be used for the conversation. The lower area contains information about you.

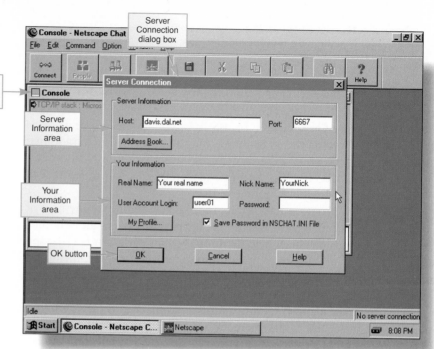

FIGURE 3-65

3 **Click the Host text box. Type** us.undernet.org **in the text box. This is the domain name of an IRC server computer.**

The new domain name replaces davis.dal.net (Figure 3-66). The number 6667 in the Port text box should not be changed. This identifies which of the computer's port numbers to contact. IRC is assigned to port 6667.

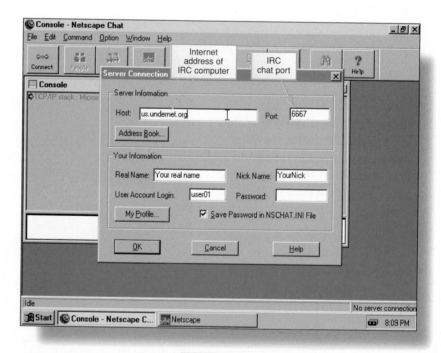

FIGURE 3-66

4 Press the TAB key to move the insertion point to the Real Name text box in the Your Information area and then type your full name in the text box. Press the TAB key to move to the nickname text box and then type in the name you want to use to identify your comments. Be sure to replace the name kurtj with your own nickname. Press the TAB key and then type your nickname in the User Account Login and Password text boxes. These entries are used for those IRC computers that require user names and passwords. The IRC server you are using in this project does not use user names and passwords, but the NetChat program will not continue without something in these text boxes.

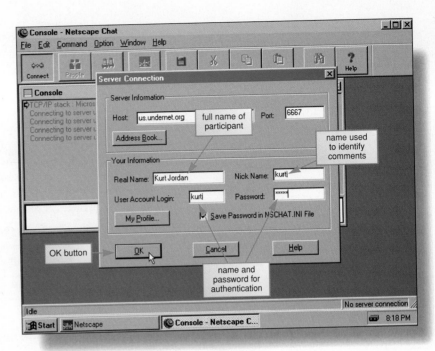

FIGURE 3-67

The Server Connection dialog box contains all the information needed to contact the IRC server computer and connect to IRC using a nickname (Figure 3-67).

5 Click the OK button to initiate the connection.

The Server Connection dialog box disappears, and a Connecting to server dialog box briefly displays, indicating a connection to the server is being established. When the connection is made, instructions for using IRC display in the Console window (Figure 3-68).

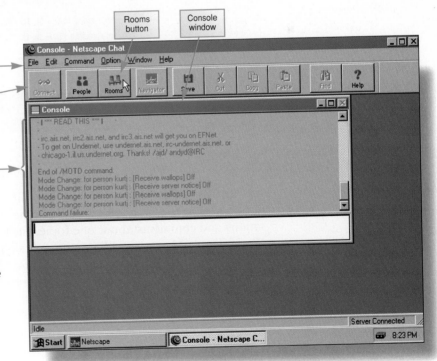

FIGURE 3-68

Other Ways

1. Click Connect button
2. Press ALT+F, press ALT+O

More *About* **the Console Window**

IRC commands can be entered in the text box at the bottom of the Console window. Some IRC commands are /help, /list and /join.

The Console window will display information about the status of your IRC connection. The Netscape Chat window contains a menu bar and a toolbar containing buttons that perform frequently requested activities. Table 3-6 shows the buttons and their functions.

TABLE 3-6

BUTTON	FUNCTION
Connect	Displays the Server Connection dialog box that you use to specify which chat server you want to contact. You must specify your connection by its Internet host name, port, and your personal user information.
People	Displays the Show People dialog box that you use to select the person you want to communicate with, or obtain more information on. Clicking this button is the same as choosing Show People on the File menu.
Rooms	Displays the Conversation Rooms dialog box that you use to start or join a room. Clicking this button is the same as choosing Show Rooms on the File menu.
Navigator	Opens and closes the Chat URL toolbar. Clicking this button is the same as choosing Show Toolbar on the Browser menu.
Save	Saves the contents of the transcript pane to a text file. Clicking this button is the same as choosing Save transcript on the Edit menu.
Cut	Removes the highlighted text from the Notepad. Clicking this button is the same as choosing Cut on the Edit menu.
Copy	Copies the highlighted text in your Notepad to the Clipboard. Clicking this button is the same as choosing Copy on the Edit menu.
Paste	Inserts the copied text into the new location in your Notepad. Clicking this button is the same as choosing Paste on the Edit menu.
Find	Searches text strings in the Console or Room window.
Help	Displays the Contents page of the Netscape Chat online Help system.

Listing IRC Channels

The IRC server computer has many different conversations occurring at once. Each conversation is called a **room**. Like newsgroups, each room contains conversations and comments about one topic, such as atheism, cave dwellers or *As The World Turns*. Most rooms have a pound sign (#) as the first character. You can join an existing room or create a new room. One of the toolbar buttons lists all the available rooms. Follow the next step to list the IRC rooms.

Steps **To List IRC Channels**

1 **Click the Rooms button.**

The Conversation Rooms dialog box displays (Figure 3-69). This dialog box contains a Room text box, which is similar to a bookmark list, where rooms you join are stored. Option buttons control the type of conversation to join. The list of rooms contains the name of the room, how many persons have joined the room, and a brief comment describing the topic of discussion in the room.

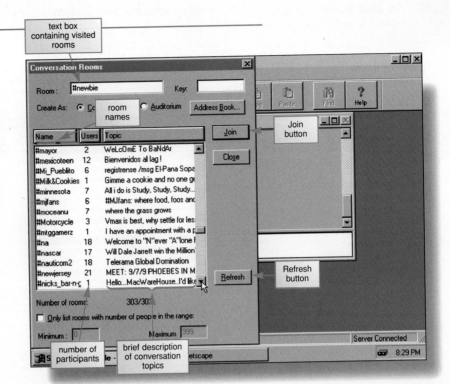

FIGURE 3-69

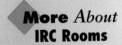

The Conversation Rooms dialog box allows you to scroll through the list of rooms. Command buttons allow you to join a discussion, close the dialog box, and refresh the list. Remember that new rooms can be created. Once the list of rooms has displayed, you can click one and then participate in live conversations.

Joining an IRC Room

Joining an ongoing conversation is as easy as clicking the room you wish to join. The steps on the next page show how to join a room and participate in a real-time conversation with the people in room #newbie, a room for new IRC users.

Other Ways

1. Press ALT+F, press ALT+R

More *About* IRC Rooms

You can eliminate those rooms with only one or two participants by changing the settings at the bottom of the Conversation Rooms dialog box.

Steps To Join an IRC Room

1 **Scroll down the list of IRC rooms until the #newbie room displays. Click the #newbie entry in the list.**

The #newbie room becomes highlighted (Figure 3-70). Nine other people currently are in the room.

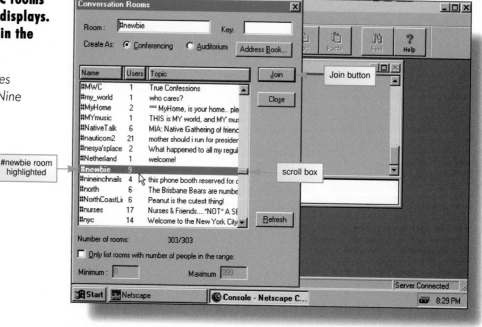

FIGURE 3-70

2 **Click the Join button.**

The Conferencing: #newbie window displays (Figure 3-71). The window contains two panes, a text box, and the URL area. The members pane contains the nicknames of the persons who have joined the room. The transcript pane contains the comments and pieces of conversation that participants send to the room. In the Notepad text box, you can type your comments and enter IRC commands. The URL area contains buttons and a URL drop-down list box for saving interesting URLs. You now are ready to talk to other people in the room.

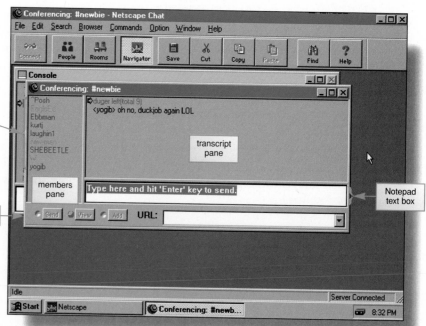

FIGURE 3-71

Netscape Navigator 3 **Windows 95**

NetChat • NN 3.47

Figure 3-71 shows nine people in this room: Posh, EagleEd, Ebbman, kurtj, laughin1, saw-man, SHEBEETLE, W, and yogib. Anything that is typed by any of the other people will display in the transcript pane on each of their screens.

Conversing on an IRC Room

When you join an IRC room, it is customary to say hello. The next steps show how to participate in an IRC conversation.

 Steps **To Converse on an IRC Room**

1 **Click the Notepad text box to obtain an insertion point. Type** hello **in the text box.**

The text displays in the text box (Figure 3-72). You can use the cursor keys to correct any typing errors that may occur. Notice T-slippen just entered the room shown in Figure 3-72.

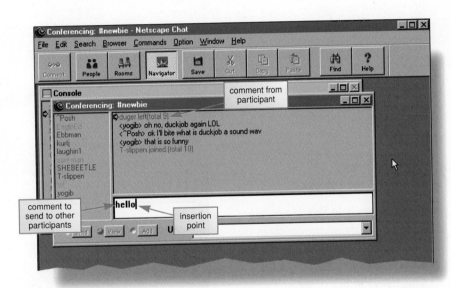

FIGURE 3-72

2 **Press the ENTER key.**

The line you typed displays in the transcript pane (Figure 3-73). Notice it is prefaced with your nickname. The other participants also can see the line. When someone types a line, it displays on your screen. Figure 3-73 shows a response to your comment from laughin1. You can respond to the comments by entering another line of text.

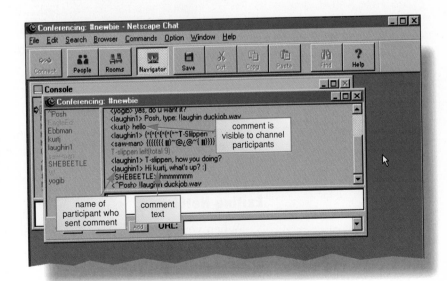

FIGURE 3-73

You can continue with the conversation in this manner, reading what other people have to say and entering your own responses.

Switching to Another Room

As easily as you joined the #newbie room, you can switch to another room. The following steps show how to leave the #newbie room and join a different room.

Steps **To Switch to Another Room**

1 **Click the Close button.**

The Conferencing window disappears (Figure 3-74). You can see the status messages in the Console window indicating you have left the room.

2 **Click the Rooms button on the toolbar.**

The Conversation Rooms window displays, as shown previously in Figure 3-69 on page NN 3.45. You can click another room and then click the Join button to join the room.

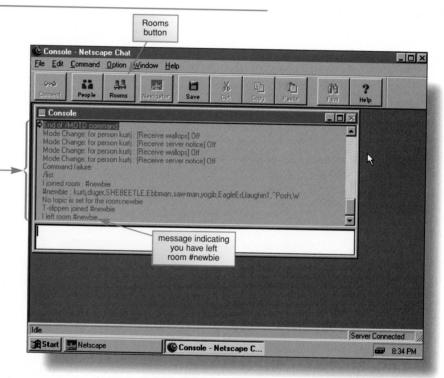

Rooms button

IRC status information

message indicating you have left room #newbie

FIGURE 3-74

You now can participate in the current discussion topic in the new IRC room you just joined. Similar to WebChat, NetChat is unregulated and people can say whatever they please.

Exiting NetChat

When you are finished using NetChat, you can exit, as show in the following steps.

Steps To Exit NetChat

1 On the menu bar click File.

The File menu displays (Figure 3-75). Notice you can disconnect without exiting. This allows you to establish a connection to another IRC server computer and talk to different people. Appendix A contains the URL of a Web page listing the Internet addresses of other IRC servers you can contact.

2 Click Exit.

The Windows 95 desktop displays.

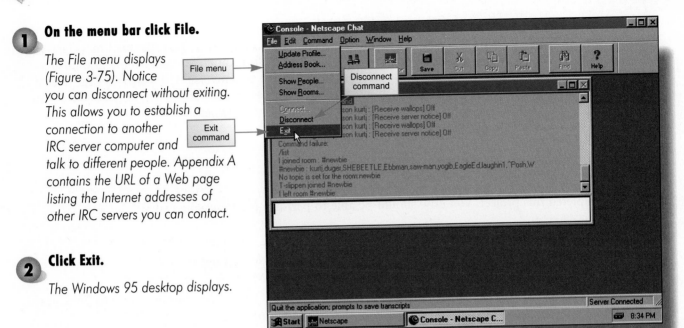

FIGURE 3-75

> **Other Ways**
> 1. Click Close button

You have learned how to connect to an IRC server computer and engage in live conversations with other people on the World Wide Web using NetChat.

> **More** *About* **NetChat Conversations**
>
> You can copy pieces of conversations to the Clipboard and paste the pieces into other Windows 95 applications.

Project Summary

In finishing this project, you now are prepared to assist Milschester Library patrons in preparing Netscape for use with electronic mail. Techniques for sending, receiving, and managing electronic mail messages were presented. You learned how to send and read newsgroup articles. Procedures for subscribing and unsubscribing to and from newsgroups were explained. You learned how to converse with others on the World Wide Web using WebChat. Connecting to an Internet Relay Chat server was discussed. Finally, you learned how to join an IRC room and carry on live conversations with other Internet users.

What You Should Know

Having completed this project, you now should be able to perform the following tasks:

- Access Electronic Mail Using Netscape *(NN 3.8)*
- Access Newsgroups in Netscape *(NN 3.25)*
- Add an Address to the Address Book *(NN 3.20)*
- Connect to a WebChat Session *(NN 3.37)*
- Contact the Mail Server *(NN 3.14)*
- Converse on an IRC Room *(NN 3.47)*
- Converse on WebChat *(NN 3.39)*
- Delete a Mail Message *(NN 3.18)*
- Display All Available Newsgroups *(NN 3.26)*
- Display the Address Book *(NN 3.19)*
- Display the rec.animals.wildlife Newsgroup *(NN 3.28)*
- Exit Electronic Mail *(NN 3.23)*
- Exit NetChat *(NN 3.49)*
- Exit Netscape *(NN 3.41)*
- Exit Netscape News *(NN 3.36)*
- Join an IRC Room *(NN 3.46)*

- List IRC Channels *(NN 3.45)*
- Post a Newsgroup Article *(NN 3.22)*
- Print a Mail Message *(NN 3.17)*
- Provide Your E-Mail Information to Netscape *(NN 3.6)*
- Read a Mail Message in Netscape *(NN 3.15)*
- Read a Newsgroup Article *(NN 3.29)*
- Read the Next Newsgroup Article *(NN 3.30)*
- Save a Mail Message on a Floppy Disk *(NN 3.16)*
- Send a Mail Message *(NN 3.11)*
- Start Netscape *(NN 3.5)*
- Start the NetChat Program *(NN 3.41)*
- Subscribe to a Newsgroup *(NN 3.34)*
- Switch to Another Room *(NN 3.48)*
- Unsubscribe from a Newsgroup *(NN 3.35)*
- Use the Address Book When Composing a Message *(NN 3.22)*

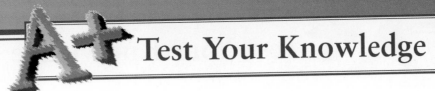 **Test Your Knowledge**

1 True/False

Instructions: Circle T if the statement is true or F if the statement is false.

T F   1. Mail messages must be read in the order they appear in the Inbox folder.

T F   2. An electronic mail address consists of an individual's account name, followed by the & character, and then the Internet address or domain name of the remote computer.

T F   3. It is not important to have a good subject in your messages because very few people read the subjects.

T F   4. You generally can determine the topic of discussion you will find in a newsgroup by looking at its name.

T F   5. Sending an article to a newsgroup is called subscribing.

T F   6. New newsgroups are being created everyday.

T F   7. Newsgroups allow live, ongoing conversations.

T F   8. IRC was created only recently as a World Wide Web service.

T F   9. Individual conversations in IRC are called stations.

T F 10. WebChat and NetChat conversations are moderated to prevent objectionable comments from appearing.

2 Multiple Choice

Instructions: Circle the correct response.

1. The place where mail messages are stored until they are read is called _____.
   a. a thread
   b. a floppy disk
   c. newsrc
   d. a mail box

2. Special combinations of characters called _____ help convey emotion and personality.
   a. abbreviations
   b. smileys
   c. frowns
   d. remarks

3. A(n) _____ is a preserved record of your mail correspondence.
   a. audit trail
   b. file on a floppy disk
   c. thread
   d. mail box

(continued)

Test Your Knowledge

Multiple Choice *(continued)*

4. The collection of computers that store and make available newsgroups is called _____.
   a. a thread
   b. an FTP archive
   c. Usenet
   d. the Internet

5. Access to newsgroups is achieved by clicking the _____.
   a. Newsgroups button
   b. Window menu
   c. Back button
   d. Net Directory button

6. Adding a newsgroup to the newsrc file is called _____.
   a. unsubscribing
   b. subscribing
   c. posting
   d. saving

7. To receive a fresh copy of a form being used for live conversations, _____.
   a. click the Print button on the toolbar
   b. press the ALT + TAB keys
   c. click the Forward button on the toolbar
   d. click the specially designated button on the form

8. A _____ is used to identify your comments in NetChat.
   a. nickname
   b. picture
   c. Chat button
   d. room

9. Individual conversations taking place in Internet Relay Chat (IRC) are called _____.
   a. nicknames
   b. stations
   c. rooms
   d. panes

10. The display area in mail and newsgroups is divided into areas called _____.
    a. channels
    b. panes
    c. text boxes
    d. dialog boxes

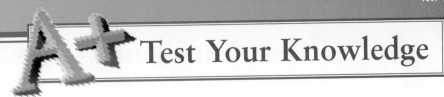

Test Your Knowledge

3 Understanding Netscape's Electronic Mail Preferences Sheets

Instructions: Figures 3-76 and 3-77 show Netscape's e-mail Servers and Identity sheets. Write in the appropriate text boxes the entries necessary for identifying your e-mail account and the location of your Inbox folder.

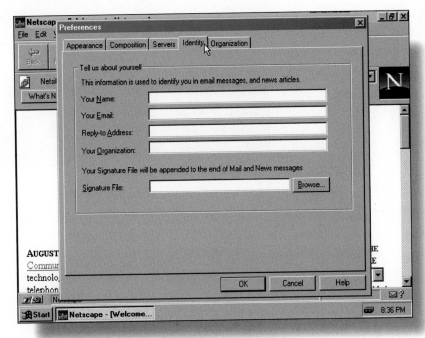

FIGURE 3-76

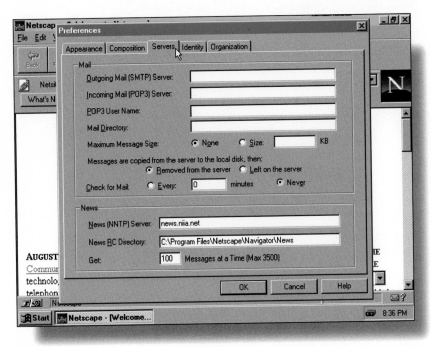

FIGURE 3-77

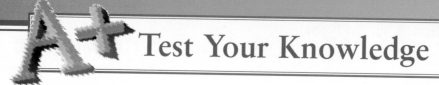

Test Your Knowledge

4 Understanding How to Delete Electronic Mail Messages

Instructions: Figure 3-78 shows the Netscape Mail window with a sample mail message displayed. In the spaces provided, write the steps to permanently delete the sample mail message.

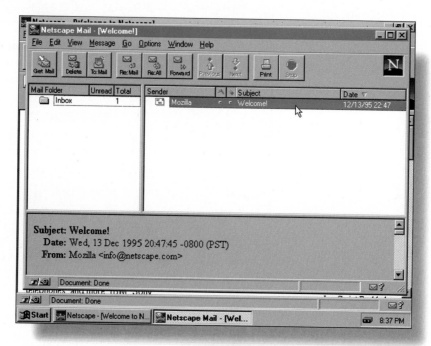

FIGURE 3-78

1. _____
2. _____
3. _____
4. _____
5. _____
6. _____

Use Help

1 Setting Newsgroups Preferences

Instructions: Start Netscape and perform the following tasks with a computer:

Just as it is possible to save your bookmarks and electronic mail folders on a diskette so you can use them on any computer running Netscape, so you can also save your list of subscribed newsgroups to a diskette. Using Netscape Help, display information describing the preference setting for the location of the subscribed newsgroup file. Print the page and turn it in to your instructor.

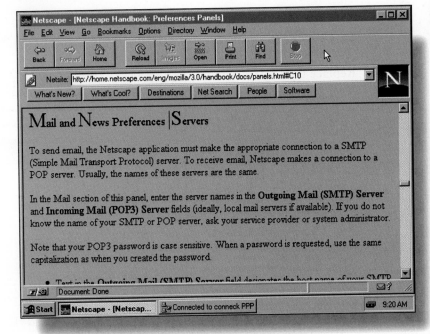

FIGURE 3-79

2 Sorting Mail Messages

Instructions: Start Netscape and perform the following tasks with a computer:

There will be times you will receive messages from several individuals. Scrolling through the message heading pane picking only the messages from one person can be tedious. It is possible to sort the messages in the heading pane in several different ways. Using Netscape Help, find out how to sort the messages in the heading page by sender name. Print the page containing the instructions for sorting messages in the heading pane and turn it in to your instructor.

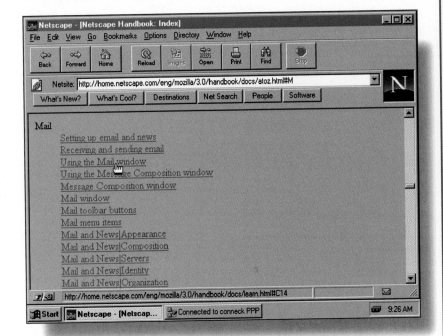

FIGURE 3-80

In the Lab

1 Sending Electronic Mail Messages

Instructions: Start Netscape and perform the following tasks with a computer:

1. Replace the URL in the location text box with http://www.house.gov and retrieve the page.

2. Find and display the electronic mail address of the member of the House of Representatives from your district. If your representative is not listed, select the name of one you recognize.

3. Bring up the Message Composition window as shown in Figure 3-81.

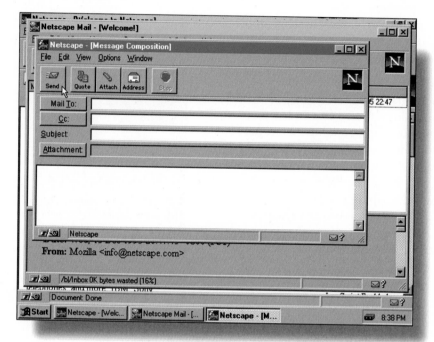

FIGURE 3-81

4. Using the electronic mail address of the U.S. House of Representative member you obtained in Step 2, compose a mail message to your representative about some issue that is important to you.

5. Send a carbon copy of the message to your instructor. Ask your instructor for his or her electronic mail address and enter it in the Cc text box. If sending a copy to your instructor is not possible, send a copy to yourself, print the copy you receive, using the same technique for printing a Web page, and turn it in to your instructor.

2 Reading Newsgroup Articles

Instructions: Start Netscape and perform the following tasks with a computer:

1. Display the News window.
2. Retrieve the list of all the available newsgroups (Figure 3-82).
3. Select a newsgroup that interests you.
4. Select one of the articles in the newsgroup to read.
5. Print the article, write your name on it, and turn it in to your instructor.

In the Lab

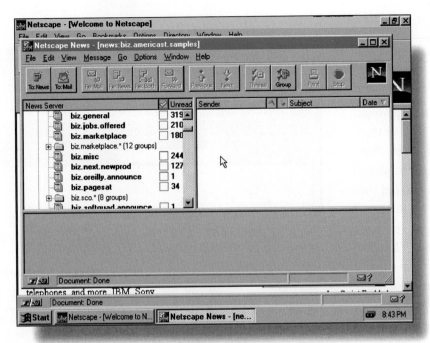

FIGURE 3-82

3 Posting Newsgroup Articles

Instructions: Start Netscape and perform the following tasks with a computer:

1. Display the News window.
2. Retrieve the list of all the available newsgroups.
3. Select the news.misc newsgroup from the list of newsgroups.
4. Bring up the Message Composition window as shown in Figure 3-83.
5. Compose and send a test article to the news.misc newsgroup.
6. Re-display the list of articles in the news.misc newsgroup so your article displays in the summary list.
7. Display your article.
8. Print your article, write your name on it, and turn it in to your instructor.

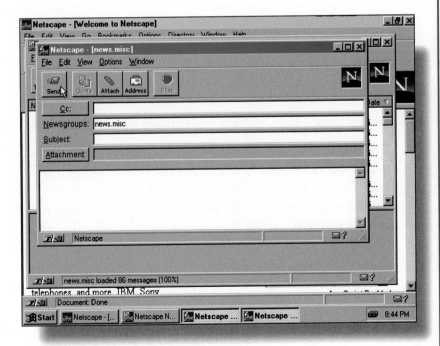

FIGURE 3-83

In the Lab

4 Conversing with WebChat

Instructions: Start Netscape and perform the following tasks with a computer:

1. Use the URL http://bip. concept.se/index4.htm to connect to WebChat.
2. Supply a name to identify your comments and then display the WebChat page.
3. Scroll down the page to reveal the form (Figure 3-84).
4. Engage someone in conversation. Find out from what part of the world he or she is participating.
5. Print the Web page containing some of your comments, write your name on it, and turn it in to your instructor.

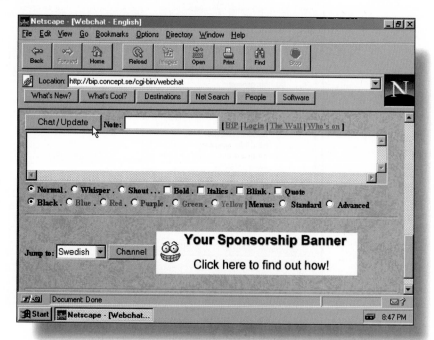

FIGURE 3-84

5 Conversing with Netscape Chat

Instructions: Start NetChat and perform the following tasks with a computer:

1. Connect to the us.undernet.org IRC server by clicking the Connect button on the toolbar.
2. Display the list of rooms using the Group button (Figure 3-85).
3. Choose an interesting room to join.
4. Engage someone in conversation. Find out from what part of the world he or she is participating.
5. Print the transcript of your conversation using the Print button on the toolbar, write your name on the printout, and turn it in to your instructor.

In the Lab

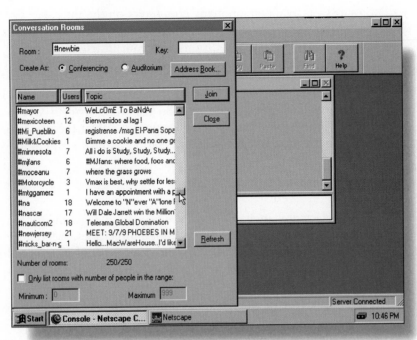

FIGURE 3-85

6 Connecting to the Shelly Cashman Online Home Page

Instructions: Additional exercises for this project are available at the Shelly Cashman Online World Wide Web site. Perform the following steps to access these exercises. With Netscape on the screen, click the location text box. Type http://www.scseries.com/ in the location text box and then press the ENTER key. Scroll down and click Shelly Cashman Student Center. Scroll down and click Netscape 3 for Windows 95. Scroll down and click Project 3 Conversing Over the Internet. Complete the activities listed.

Cases and Places

The difficulty of these case studies varies:

▶ Case studies preceded by a single half moon are the least difficult. You are asked to perform the exercise based on techniques learned in the project.

▶▶ Case studies preceded by two half moons are more difficult. You must perform the exercise and carry out calculations.

▶▶▶ Case studies preceded by three half moons are the most difficult. You must perform the exercise by obtaining and organizing the necessary information and then prepare a report.

Cases and Places

1 ▸ Internet Relay Chat, or IRC, is available on many computers on the Internet. Using Netscape, display the Netscape News window and find any newsgroups dealing with IRC. Display and print one of the more interesting articles you find there and turn it in to your instructor.

2 ▸ In addition to IRC sites, WebChat sites are emerging on the Web. Using a Web search engine, compile a list of several WebChat and IRC sites. Try connecting to one of the sites. Engage someone in conversation at the site. Print a transcript of your conversation and turn it in along with the list of sites to your instructor.

3 ▸ Lists of persons and their electronic mail addresses are becoming available for searching on the Web. Use Netscape's People button and select one of the e-mail directories. Search for your own name. Print the page containing the results. Search for the name of one of your friends. Print the page containing the results. Search for a well-known person, such as Theodore Roosevelt. Print the results page and turn in all three pages to your instructor.

4 ▸▸ Netscape is just one of several available programs that provide access to electronic mail. Find out about two other Windows-based electronic mail programs. Compare their features with Netscape. Write a summary of your findings and turn it in to your instructor.

5 ▸▸ The Servers sheet in the Preferences dialog box of Netscape Mail and News Preferences contains references to several acronyms: SMTP; POP; NNTP; and News RC. Find out what the letters of the acronyms stand for. Write a brief description of what the four acronyms represent and turn it in to your instructor.

6 ▸▸▸ One of the more popular newsgroup programs prior to the World Wide Web is called rn. Research the rn program. Compile a list of the rn commands that correspond to Netscape News functions, such as subscribing to a newsgroup and reading an article, and turn it in to your instructor.

7 ▸▸▸ One of the numerous services on the Internet is called a listserv. Find out how a listserv works. How does a listserv compare with newsgroups? Prepare a report on your findings and turn it in to your instructor.

Appendix A

Popular Web Sites

Introduction

This appendix contains the URLs for interesting and useful Web sites categorized by topic. Each URL entry contains a brief description of what you can find at the site. At the end of the appendix is a list of public access FTP and gopher sites. You also can obtain additional URLs for popular Web sites by accessing the Student Center on the Shelly Cashman Online Web page at http://www.scseries.com.

ART	Art on the Net	http://www.art.net/
	Original Watercolor Paintings	http://www.fine-art.com/colorado/ga01000.html
	Spy photographs	http://edcwww.cr.usgs.gov/dclass/dclass.html

BUSINESS	Fidelity Investments®/Mutual Funds	http://www.fid-inv.com
	Small Business Administration	http://www.sba.gov
	NETworth	http://www.galt.com
	U.S. Securities & Exchange Commission	http://www.sec.gov

ENTERTAIN-MENT	CBS Eye on the Net	http://www.cbs.com/
	News on TV shows from all the networks	http://www.TV.net
	Movies	http://www.movieweb.com/movie/movie.html

GOVERNMENT	FedWorld government information source	http://www.fedworld.gov
	The Legal Information Institute	http://www.law.cornell.edu
	U.S. Patent database	http://town.hall.org/patent/patent.html
	U.S. Senate	http://www.senate.gov
	U.S. Geological Survey	http://info.er.usgs.gov

| INTERNET RELAY CHAT | Chat 1 | http://ca.undernet.org |
| | Chat 2 | http://www.irsociety.com/webchat.html |

JOBS	Career Fair for College Graduates	http://www.monster.com
	CareerMosaic®	http://www.careermosaic.com
	Careers in Academe	http://chronicle.merit.edu
	CareerWEB	http://www.cweb.com

MISCELLANEOUS	Dinosaurs	http://www.utdallas.edu/dept/geoscience/dinosaur
	Internet Millionaires Page	http://www.pulver.com/million
	Planet Earth home page	http://white.nosc.mil/info_modern.html
	Bartlett's Familiar Quotations	http://www.cc.columbia.edu/acis/bartleby/bartlett
	Rolling Stones Web Site	http://www.stones.com

MUSEUMS	Chicago Field Museum of Natural History	http://rs6000.bvis.uic.edu/museum
	Chicago Museum of Science and Industry	http://www.msichicago.org
	Interactive Natural History Museum	http://www.ucmp.berkeley.edu

MUSIC	RockWeb pages for bands	http://www.rock.net
	Ticketmaster	http://www.ticketmaster.com
	Sample sound files of various bands	http://www.iuma.com

NEWS/PERIODICALS	Life magazine online	http://pathfinder.com/Life
	Wired magazine online	http://www.wired.com
	Web Review Magazine	http://www.gnn.com/wr/
	Online news	http://www.cnn.com
	The Wall Street Journal Interactive Edition	http://www.wsj.com

| SHOPPING | Internet Shopping Network | http://www.internet.net/directories.html |
| | World Wide Web Shopping Directory | http://worldshopping.com/direct.html |

SPORTS	Baseball	http://www.fastball.com
	Basketball	http://www.nba.com
	Boxing	http://www.sportsline.com/u/boxing/index.html
	Football	http://www.sportsbeat.com

FTP SITES	Games	ftp://ftp.wustl.edu/pub/windows_uploads/games
	Electronic books	ftp://ftp.spies.com
	Pictures and sound files	ftp://sunsite.unc.edu

Index